M000213573

BUILDING MOBILE APPS AT SCALE

39 ENGINEERING CHALLENGES

GERGELY OROSZ

Copyright © 2021 by Gergely Orosz

All rights reserved.

No part of this book may be reproduced or used in any manner without written permission of the copyright owner except for the use of quotations in a book review. For more information, please address: scale@pragmaticengineer.com.

ISBN: 978-1-63877-886-8 (paperback)

FIRST EDITION, v1.0

mobileatscale.com

CONTENTS

INTRODUCTION

I have noticed that while there is a lot of appreciation for backend and distributed systems challenges, there is often less empathy for why mobile development is hard when done at scale. Building a backend system that serves millions of customers means building highly available and scalable systems and operating these reliably. But what about the mobile clients for the same systems?

Most engineers who have not built mobile apps assume the mobile app is a simple facade that requires less engineering effort to build and operate. Having built both types of systems, I can say this is not the case. There is plenty of depth in building large, native, mobile applications, but often little curiosity from people not in this space. Product managers, business stakeholders, and even non-native mobile engineers rarely understand why it "takes so long" to ship something on mobile.

This book collects challenges engineers face when building iOS and Android apps at scale. By scale, I mean having numbers of users in the millions and being built by large engineering teams. These teams launch features continuously and still ensure the app works reliably, and in a performant way.

This book is a summary of the current industry practices used by large, native mobile teams and points to some of the common approaches to tackle them. Much of the experience conveyed in this book comes from my time working at Uber on a complex and widely-used app. More than 30 other engineers working in similarly complex environments have contributed their insights; engineers building apps at the likes of Twitter, Amazon, Flipkart, Square, Capital One and many other companies.

I hope this book helps non-mobile engineers build empathy for the type of challenges and tradeoffs mobile engineers face and be a conversation starter between backend, web, and mobile teams.

ACKNOWLEDGMENTS

The book has been written with the significant input and reviews of more than 30 mobile engineers and managers, many of them deep experts in their respective fields. Thank you very much to all of them. If you are on Twitter, I suggest you follow them:

- Abhijith Krishnappa (Halodoc)
- Andrea Antonioni (Just Eat)
- Andreea Sicaru (Uber)
- Andy Boedo (RevenueCat, Elevate Labs)
- Ankush Gupta (Quizlet)
- Artem Chubaryan (Square)
- Barnabas Gema (Shapr3D)
- Barisere Jonathan (Sprinthubmobile)
- Corentin Kerisit (Zenly)
- Dan Kesack (DraftKings)
- Edu Caselles (Author: The Mobile Interview, Funding Circle)
- Emmanuel Goossaert (Booking.com)
- Franz Busch (Sixt)
- Guillermo Orellana (Monzo, Skyscanner, Badoo)

- Injy Zarif (Convoy, Microsoft)
- Jake Lee (Photobox)
- Jared Sheehan (Capital One)
- Javi Pulido (Plain Concepts)
- Jorge Coca (VG Ventures)
- Julian Harty (previously Google, eBay, Badoo, Salesforce, Klarna, ServiceNow, and others)
- Leland Takamine (perf.dev, Uber)
- Matija Grcic (EMG Consulting)
- Michael Bailey (GDE, American Express)
- Michael Sena (Tesla, Amazon)
- Nacho Lopez (Twitter, Facebook, Yahoo)
- Patrick Zearfoss (Capital One)
- Praveen Sanap (Carousell)
- Paul Razgaitis (Cameo, Braintree, Venmo)
- Robin van Dijke (Uber, Apple)
- Rui Peres (Sphere, Babylon Health)
- Sabyasachi Ruj (Flipkart, CloudMagic, Webyog)
- Sathvik Parekodi
- Tuğkan Kibar
- Tuomas Artman (Linear, Uber)
- Wouter van den Broek

Thank you to Emmanuel Goossaert for writing most of Chapter 10: Third-Party Libraries and SDKs.

Special thanks to the editor of the book, Dominic Gover at Best English Copy for helping create a book that is pleasant to read.

ABOUT THE AUTHOR

Gergely has been building native mobile apps since 2010, starting on Windows Phone, later on iOS, and Android. Starting from one-person apps, he worked with small teams at Skyscanner, to hundreds of engineers working on the same codebase at Uber.

At Uber, he worked on the Rider and Driver app rewrites, both projects involving hundreds of mobile engineers. The apps he worked on had more than 100 million monthly users in more than 60 countries, with several features built for a single country or region.

You can read books he has written, browse The Pragmatic Engineer Blog he writes and connect with him on social media channels.

twitter.com/GergelyOrosz

linkedin.com/in/gergelyorosz

youtube.com/mrgergelyorosz

SPONSORS

Publishing of this book has been sponsored by vendors providing world-class mobile engineering solutions. Using vendor solutions over building your own is often the pragmatic approach: this allows you to focus on providing business value over maintaining infrastructure.

———

Bitrise is CI/CD built for mobile - by mobile engineers. From pull request, to app store submission and beyond, Bitrise automates, monitors and improves your app development workflows. Teams who use Bitrise build better quality apps, deliver them faster, with developers who are happy.

Bitrise supports native Android or iOS, React Native, Flutter and other mobile builds. More than 100,000 developers and thousands of organizations trust Bitrise to increase productivity. Try Bitrise for free at Bitrise.io today, and build better apps, faster.

———

Bugsnag is an error monitoring and application stability management solution. Not all bugs are worth fixing, and stability is the key to making data-driven decisions on whether to build software or to fix bugs.

Bugsnag is a daily stability dashboard for mobile engineers, product managers, release managers, and observability teams to manage quality applications. We help drive code ownership, balance faster release cycles, reduce technical debt, and improve user experience.

Processing over a billion crash reports a day, Bugsnag is used by over 6,000 of the world's best small and large engineering teams such as Airbnb, Slack, Square, Lyft, Shopify and Tinder. Get started for free today at Bugsnag.com.

———

SonarSource builds world-class code quality and security tools used by more than 200,000 engineering teams. Open-source and commercial code products that help you find and fix bugs, vulnerabilities and code smells, so you deliver better mobile apps.

SonarCloud is the leading code static analysis and code security tool, integrating with GitHub, GitLab and other providers. It integrates directly into your code review workflow, and helps assess your code health. Free to use for open source projects - get started at SonarQube.org.

SonarQube is the on-premise code quality and security tool supporting Swift, Kotlin, Objective C, Java, and 24 other languages. Detect code smells, common bugs, and security hotspots. Get started for free at SonarCloud.io.

———

RevenueCat makes it easy to build and manage iOS and Android in-app purchases at scale. With a few lines of code RevenueCat provides IAP infrastructure, customer analytics, data integrations, and gives you time back from dealing with edge cases and updates across the platforms.

Created by developers, for developers, thousands of the world's best apps use RevenueCat to power their in-app purchases and subscriptions. Get started for free at RevenueCat.com.

———

TouchLab is trusted by mobile innovators to scale Kotlin Multiplatform Mobile (KMM). Touchlab accelerates KMM adoption through product & SDK development, early adopter support, architectural & production-readiness reviews and open-source projects.

TouchLab advises enterprises like Square and NBC on scaling KMM and partners with JetBrains to increase KMM adoption. Looking to get started with KMM? Check out their Kotlin Multiplatform starter kit at Touchlab.co.

———

Perf.dev is an industry-leading mobile performance platform and enables a proactive workflow for managing mobile performance.

The platform provides automated testing and root cause analysis to address performance issues before releasing to end-users. Upgrade your mobile performance strategy at perf.dev.

———

Craft Docs is the modern writing app, native for MacOS, iPhone and iPad, built with Catalyst. Perfect from note-taking to collaborating within a team. Most people who try Craft say the same: that this is the app they've been looking for all this time. Try Craft for free at Craft.do

WHEN THINGS ARE SIMPLE

Let's address the elephant in the room: the frequent assumption that client-side development is simple. The assumption that the biggest complexity lies in making sure things look good on various mobile devices.

When the problem you are solving is simple, and the scope is small, it is easier to come up with simple solutions. When you are building an app with limited functionality with a small team and very few users, your mobile app should not be complicated. Your backend will likely be easy to understand. Your website will be a no-brainer. You can use existing libraries, templates, and all sorts of shortcuts to put working solutions in place.

Once you grow in size — customers, engineers, codebase and features — everything becomes more complex, more bloated, and harder to understand and modify, including the mobile codebase. This is the part we focus on in this book; when things become complex. When your app gets big, there are no silver bullets that will magically solve all of your pain points, only tough tradeoffs to make.

This book begins at the point at which your app stops being simple.

PART I

CHALLENGES DUE TO THE NATURE OF MOBILE APPLICATIONS

People who have not done mobile development often assume that most challenges of native apps are similar to those on the web.

This could not be further from reality.

Mobile engineering has close to a dozen unique challenges that exist neither on the web, nor on the backend. Most of these relate to the binary distribution of mobile apps; the need to work in low connectivity setups, and to incorporate unique capabilities like push notifications, deeplinks or in-app purchases.

In this part, we will go through the challenges that are new to people who have not worked in the mobile domain, both for software engineers, but also for engineering managers, product managers and business stakeholders.

1

STATE MANAGEMENT

State management is the root of most headaches for native mobile development, similar to modern web and backend development. The difference with mobile apps is how app lifecycle events and transitions are not a cause for concern in the web and backend world. Examples of the app-level lifecycle transitions are the app pausing and going to the background, then returning to the foreground or being suspended. The states are similar, but not identical for iOS and Android.

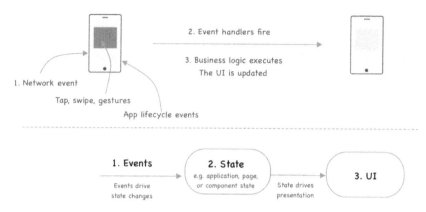

Events driving state changes in mobile apps

Events drive state changes in most mobile apps. These events trigger in asynchronous ways such as application state changes, network requests or user input. Most bugs and unexpected crashes are usually caused by an unexpected or untested combination of events and the application's state becoming corrupted. State becoming corrupted is a common problem area with apps where global or local states are manipulated by multiple components unknown to each other. Teams that run into this issue start to isolate component and application state as much as possible and tend to start using reactive state management sooner or later.

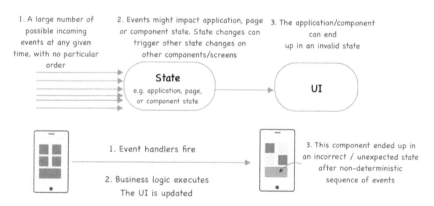

A common root reason for exotic bugs in complex apps: non-deterministic events put parts of the app in invalid states

Reactive programming is a preferred method for dealing with a large and stateful app, in order to isolate state changes. You keep state as immutable as possible, storing models as immutable objects that emit state changes. This is the practice used at Uber, is the approach Airbnb takes, and is how N26 built their app. Though the approach can be tedious in propagating state changes down a tree of components, the same tediousness makes it difficult to make unintended state changes in unrelated components.

Applications sharing the same resources with all other apps, and the OS killing apps at short notice, are two of the biggest differences between developing for mobile versus developing for other platforms, like backend and the web. The OS monitors *OS* CPU, memory, and energy consumption. If the OS determines that *Kills* your app is taking up too many resources in the foreground or the background, then it can be killed with little warning. It is the app *app* developer's responsibility to react to application state changes, save state, and to restore the app to where it was running. On iOS, this means handling app states and transitions between them. On Android, you need to react to changes in the Activity lifecycle.

Global application state, such as permissions, Bluetooth and connectivity state, and others, brings an interesting set of challenges. Whenever one of these global states changes, for example, the network connectivity drops, then different parts of the app might need to react differently.

With global state, the challenge becomes deciding which component owns listening to these state changes. At one end of the spectrum, application screens or components could listen to global state changes they care about; resulting in lots of code duplication, but components handling all of the global state concerns. At the other end, a component could listen to certain global state changes and forward these on to specific parts of the application. This might result in less complex code, but now there is a tight coupling between the global state handler and the components it knows.

App launch points like deeplinks or internal shortcut navigation points within the app also add complexity to state management. With deeplinks, the application state might need to be set up after the deeplink is activated. We will go into more detail in the Deeplinks chapter.

Resources for this chapter:
go.mobileatscale.com/1

2

MISTAKES ARE HARD TO REVERT

Mobile apps are distributed as binaries. Once a user updates to a version with a client-side bug, they are stuck with that bug until a new version is released and the user updates.

Multiple challenges come with this approach:

- **Both Apple and Google are strict on allowing executable code to be sent to apps.** Apple does not allow executing code that changes functionality in their store guidelines and Google can flag unrelated executable code as malware, as per their program policy. This means you cannot just remotely update apps. However, pushing bug fixes that revert broken functionality should be within both stores' policies: for example, when using feature flags. At the same time, Apple does allow executing non-native code like JavaScript, which is why solutions like Codepush are gaining popularity. Codepush allows React Native or Cordova apps to deliver updates on the fly. At Uber, we built a homegrown solution along the same lines, as several other companies have done.
- **It takes from hours to days to release** a new app

7

version on the store. For iOS, manual reviews happen for all apps, taking 24-48 hours to complete. Historically, every review had the possibility of rejection. As of June 2020, Apple has changed guidelines, so bug fixes are no longer delayed over guideline violations, except for legal issues. On Android, manual reviews do not always happen, but when they do, they can take more than seven days.

- **Users take days to update to the latest version** after a new version is published to the app store. This lag is true even for users with automated updates turned on.
- **You can not assume that all users will get this updated version, ever**. Some users might have automated updates disabled. Even when they update, they might skip several versions.

Chuck Rossi, part of release engineering at Facebook, summarizes what it is like to release for mobile on a Software Engineering Daily podcast episode:

"It was the most terrifying thing to take 10,000 diffs, package it into effectively a bullet, fire that bullet at the horizon and that bullet, once it leaves the barrel, it's gone. I cannot get it back, and it flies flat and true with no friction and no gravity till the heat death of the universe. It's gone. I can't fix it."

This means that all previous versions of your app need to be supported indefinitely and in theory, you should do this. The only exception is if you put homegrown controls in place and build a force update mechanism to limit the past versions to support. Android supports in-app updates in the Play Core library. iOS does not have similar native support. We will cover more on this in the Forced Upgrading chapter.

Force update

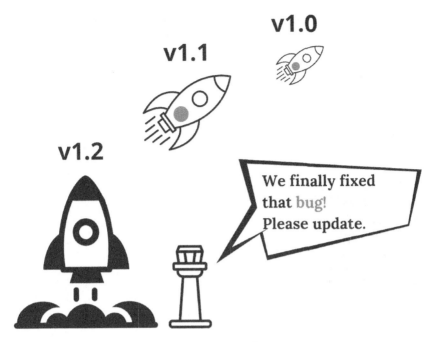

Fixing a bug in a mobile app

Assuming you have an app with millions of users, what steps can you take to minimize bugs or regressions from occurring in old versions?

- **Do thorough testing** at all levels. Automated testing, manual testing, and consider beta testing with easy feedback loops. A common approach at many companies is to release the beta app to company employees and beta users for it to "bake" for a week, collecting feedback on any issues.
- **Have a feature flagging system** in place, so you can revert bugs on the fly. Still, feature flags add further pain points. We will discuss these points in the Feature Flag Hell chapter.
- **Consider gradual rollouts**, with monitoring to ensure things work as expected. We will cover this topic in the Analytics, Monitoring and Alerting chapter.

- **Force upgrading** is a robust solution, but you will need to put one in place, and some customers might churn as a result. We will go deeper on this in the Forced Upgrading chapter.

Resources for this chapter:
go.mobileatscale.com/2

3

THE LONG TAIL OF OLD APP VERSIONS

Old versions of the app will stay around for a long time, up to several years. This time frame is only shorter if you are one of the few teams that put strict force app upgrade policies in place. Apps that have a rolling window of force upgrades include Whatsapp and Messenger. Several others use force upgrades frequently, like banking apps Monzo or American Express.

While most users will update to new app versions in a matter of days, there will be a long tail of users who are several versions behind. Some users disable automatic updates on purpose, but many who do not update are blocked because of old phones or OSes. At the same time, old app versions are unlikely to be regularly tested by the mobile team because it is a lot of effort, with little payoff.

Even a non-breaking backend change can break an older version of the app - such as changing the content of a specific response. A few practices you can do to avoid this breakage:

- **Build sturdy network response handling and parsing, using dedicated tooling** that solves these problems. I prefer strongly typed, generated contracts between client and backend like Thrift, GraphQL, or other solutions with code generation, over REST interfaces that you need to validate manually, which is bound to break when someone forgets to update the parsing logic on mobile.

- **Plan well in advance for breaking backend changes.** Have an open communications channel with the backend team. Have a way to test old app versions. Consider building new endpoints and not retiring old ones until a forced upgrade moves all current app users off the old endpoint.

- **Version your backend endpoints** and create new versions to accommodate breaking changes. When making breaking changes, you will usually create a new endpoint and mark the existing one as deprecated. Note that in case of using GraphQL, this might not apply, as GraphQL takes a strong stance against versioning.

- **Proceed with caution when deprecating endpoints** on the backend. Monitor the traffic, and have a migration plan on how to channel requests, if needed.

- **Track usage stats on an app version level.** What percentage of users is lagging three or more versions behind? Once you have this data, it is easier to decide how much effort to dedicate towards ensuring the experience works well on older versions.

- **Put client-side monitoring and alerting in place.** These alerts might be channeled to a dedicated mobile on-call, or just the normal on-call. We will dive more into this in the Analytics, Monitoring and Alerting chapter.

- **Consider doing upgrade testing**, at least for major updates. Upgrade testing is expensive, hard to automate, and there might be several permutations to try. Teams rarely do it because of this overhead.

4

DEEPLINKS

Deeplinking — providing a web or device link that opens a part of the app — becomes a surprisingly tricky problem on mobile platforms. Both iOS and Android offer APIs to deal with this, but without any opinionated native frameworks or recommended approaches. As Alberto De Bortoli puts it in the article iOS deeplinking at scale:

> "Deep linking is one of the most underestimated problems to solve on mobile."

There are a few things that make deeplinking challenging:

- **Backward compatibility:** ensuring that existing deeplinks keep working in older versions of the app, even after significant navigation or logic changes.

- **State problems when deeplinking to a running app with existing state**. Say you have an app open and are on a detail page. You tap on a deeplink in your mail app that points to another detail page. What should happen? Would the new detail page be added to the navigation stack, preserving your current state? Or should the state be reset? The solution that results in the least amount of non-deterministic behavior is to reset the app's state fully when receiving a deeplink. However, there might be flows that you do not want to break, so plan carefully.

- **iOS and Android deeplink implementation differences**. Deeplink implementations are different for iOS (universal links and URL schemes) and for Android (based on intents). There are third-party deeplink providers that supply abstractions to work with a single interface, such as Firebase Dynamic Links or Branch, among others.
- **Lack of upfront planning.** Deeplinks are often an afterthought once multiple versions of the app have shipped. However, unlike on the web, where adding links / deeplinks is more straightforward, retrofitting a deeplinking strategy can be a real engineering challenge. Deeplinks are connected to state management and the navigation architecture.

The biggest challenge with deeplinks is how neither iOS nor Android provides an opinionated approach on how to design and test deeplinks. As the number of deeplinks grows, the effort and complexity of keeping these deeplinks working snowballs. You will have to plan well ahead in building a sensible and scalable deeplink implementation.

Resources for this chapter:
go.mobileatscale.com/4

5

PUSH AND BACKGROUND NOTIFICATIONS

App push notifications are a frequently used notification, communication, and marketing tool. The business loves to use push notifications, and as a developer, you will be asked to support this method sooner or later. However, push notifications bring a set of new challenges you need to tackle.

Setting up and operating push notifications is complex. Both for Android and iOS, your app needs to obtain a token from a server (FCM on Android, APNS on iOS), then store this token on the backend. There are many steps to take to get push notifications working; see this comprehensive tutorial for iOS and this for Android.

Sending push notifications has to happen from the backend. You need to work with the backend team on the type of notifications they want to send and their triggers. Your backend counterparts will have to become familiar with the mobile push notification infrastructure and capabilities to make the most out of this channel.

Using push notifications together with emails and text messages is a popular strategy for marketing activities. In theory, such usage could go against iOS app guidelines. However, most of Apple's apps, and many third-party apps, use them as such. You will almost certainly not implement push notifications from scratch, but instead use a third-party customer engagement service like Twilio, Airship, Braze, OneSignal, or similar.

Challenges with push notifications are numerous - on top of implementing them:

- **A similar set of challenges as deeplinks,** in terms of implementing what action the notification should trigger. A push notification is a glorified deeplink: a message with an action that links into the app. Thinking about backward compatibility, state problems, and planning ahead all apply to push notifications as well.
- **Users opting out of push notifications** or not opting in. On iOS and Android, you have different ways, and limits, for detecting when this is the case. As an interesting edge case, on iOS, if a user opts out of push notifications, they can still be sent silent background notifications. Push notifications are usually a "nice to have" for many applications, exactly because you cannot guarantee that each user will opt into them, or that their device will be online to receive them.
- **Push notification delivery** is not guaranteed. Especially when sent in bulk, both Apple and Google might throttle push notifications. The rules around this throttling is a black box. However, device connectivity issues, as well as the OS restricting notifications for apps that have not recently been active, might also result in people not seeing push notifications you send.

Testing push notifications is a challenge. You can, of course, test this manually. It is more of a workaround, but you can test them on a simulator both on iOS, and on Android. However, for automated testing, you need to write end-to-end UI tests, which are expensive to create and maintain. See this tutorial on how to do this for iOS.

Background notifications are a special type of push message that is not visible for the user, but goes directly to your app. These kinds of notifications are useful to sync backend updates to the client. These notifications are called data messages on Android and background notifications on iOS. See an example for iOS usage.

The concept of background notifications is handy for real-time and multi-device scenarios. If your app is in this area, you might decide to implement a cross-platform solution for iOS and Android, and instead of the mobile app polling the server, the server sends data through background push notifications to the client. When rewriting Uber's Rider app in 2016, a major shift in our approach was exactly this; moving from poll to push, with an in-house push messaging service.

Background notifications can simplify the architecture and the business logic, but they introduce message deliverability issues, message order problems, and you need to combine this approach with local data caching for offline scenarios.

Resources for this chapter:
go.mobileatscale.com/5

6

APP CRASHES

An app crashing is one of the most noticeable bugs in any mobile app, and often ones with high business impact. Users might not complete a key flow, and they might grow frustrated and stop using the app (also known as churning), or leave poor reviews.

Crashes are not a mobile-only concern. They are a major focus area on the backend, where monitoring uncaught exceptions or 5XX status codes is common practice. On the web, due to its nature — single-threaded execution within a sandbox — crashes are rarer than on mobile apps.

track crashes

The first rule of crashes is you need to track when they happen and have sufficient debug information. Once you track crashes, you want to report on what percentage of sessions end up crashing and reduce this number as much as you can. At Uber, we tracked the crash rates from the early days, working continuously to reduce the rate of crashed sessions.

You can choose to build your own implementation of crash reporting, or use an off-the-shelf solution. As of 2021, most teams choose one of the many crash reporting solutions, such as Crashlytics or Bugsnag, for native apps.

Crashlytics
bugsnag

19

————

Bugsnag is an error monitoring and application stability management solution. Not all bugs are worth fixing, and stability is the key to making data-driven decisions on whether to build software or to fix bugs.

Bugsnag is a daily stability dashboard for mobile engineers, product managers, release managers, and observability teams to manage quality applications. Recognized for best-in-class mobile support, their diagnostic data enables engineering teams to improve application health and accelerate business growth. Bugsnag helps drive code ownership, balance faster release cycles, reduce technical debt, and improve user experience.

Processing more than a billion crash reports every day, Bugsnag is trusted by industry-leading apps such as Slack, Yelp, Lyft, Target, and Pandora. Get started for free today at Bugsnag.com.

————

On iOS, crash reports are generated on the device with every crash that you can use to map these logs to your code. Apple provides ways for developers to collect crash logs from users who opted to share this information via TestFlight or the App Store. This approach works well enough for smaller apps. On Android, Google Play also lets developers view crash stack traces through Android Vitals in the Google Play Console. As with Apple, only users who have opted in to send bug reports to developers will have these crashes logged in this portal.

Third-party or custom-built crash reporting solutions offer a few advantages on top of what the App Store and Google Play have to offer. The advantages are plenty, and most mid-sized and above apps go with either a third-party, or build a solution with the below benefits:

- **More diagnostic information.** You often want to log

additional information in your app about events that might lead to a crash.

- **Rich reporting**. Third-party solutions usually offer grouping of reports and comparison of iOS and Android crash rates.
- **Monitoring and alerting capabilities**. You can set up to get alerts when a new type of crash appears or when certain crashes spike.
- **Integrations** with the rest of the development stack. You often want to connect new crashes with your ticketing system or reference them in pull requests.

At Uber, we used third-party crash reporting from the early days. However, an in-house solution was built later. A shortcoming of many third-party crash reporting solutions is how they only collect health information on crashes and non-fatal errors, but not on app-not-responding (ANR) and memory problems. Organizations with many apps might also find the reporting not rich enough and might want to build their own reporting, to compare health statuses across many apps. Integrating better with in-house project management and coding tools could also be a reason to go custom.

Reproducibility and debuggability of crashes are other pain points that impact mobile more than backend or web teams. Especially in the Android world, users have a variety of devices that run a wide range of OS versions with a variety of app versions. If a crash can be reproduced on a simulator or on any device, you have no excuse not to fix the problem. But what if the crash only happens on specific devices?

Put a prioritization framework in place to define thresholds, above which you spend time investigating and fixing crashes. This threshold will be different based on the nature of the crash, the customer lifetime value, and other business considerations.

Frequency of users interacting part of the app that crashes:

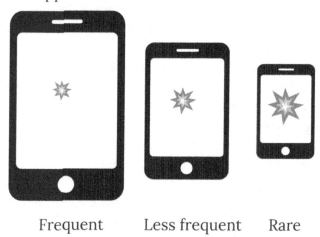

Frequent   Less frequent   Rare

How do you prioritize fixing a crash? Is a smaller crash in a more frequently used part of the app more important to fix than a larger crash in a less frequently used part?

You need to compare the cost of investigation and fixing, compared to the upside of the fix, and the opportunity cost of an engineer spending time on something else, like building revenue-generating functionality.

App stability is the metric you want to eventually measure in order to ensure that it does not regress. Your app will never be truly crash-free, but if you can reduce crashes to a stability level that means less than one in 10,000 sessions are impacted, you are on the right track. Aim to calculate an app stability score based on your total user sessions, and invest time in reducing crashes, until you meet your target.

Bugsnag have published metrics on what median app stability scores look like:

- 99.46% for apps built by 1-10 engineers
- 99.60% for apps built by 11-50 engineers
- 99.89% for apps built by 51-100 engineers

- 99.79% for apps built by 100+ engineers

If your app stability score is 99.99% or above, you are well ahead of your competition, and at what would be considered world-class reliability.

Further reading:

- Error monitoring with Bugsnag and Splunk from Zynga
- Mobile crash reporting process from LinkedIn
- The mobile crash reporting pipeline from LinkedIn (video)
- CCSM: scalable statistical anomaly detection to resolve app crashes faster from Facebook
- The path to 99.99% crash-free on iOS from Turo Engineering
- Conquering our Android crash count from Strava Engineering
- Debugging native crashes in Android apps from ProAndroidDev
- Google Maps SDK crashes, impacting hundreds of apps from Google's issue tracker
- SDKs should not crash apps - learnings from the Facebook outage from Bugsnag
- Why a small Facebook bug wreaked havoc on some of the most popular iOS apps from the Verge
- Application stability index from Bugsnag

Resources for this chapter:
go.mobileatscale.com/6

7

OFFLINE SUPPORT

Though offline support is becoming more of a feature with rich web applications, it has always been a core use case with native mobile apps. People expect apps to stay usable, even when connectivity drops. They certainly expect the state not to get lost when the signal drops or weakens.

Proper offline mode support adds a lot of complexity and unexpected edge cases to an app, such as: *hard to tell when offline*

- **Reliably detecting when the phone is offline.** The OS could report the user being online; however, this might not be the case. When the phone connects to WiFi spots that use captive portals, no data might be transmitted. For an edge case like this, the app might need to ping a couple of "always online" domains to determine this.
- **Detecting connection speed and latency** and changing the app's behaviour accordingly if it is necessary. Streaming apps will optimize the stream to match the available bandwidth. Other apps might warn users about poor connectivity that interferes with the app. Plan upfront on how you want to handle these edge cases.

- **Persisting local state when the device is offline**, and synchronizing back when the connection recovers. You need to account for race conditions when a user uses the app on multiple devices, some online, some offline. You should take additional care with app updates that modify the locally stored data, migrating the old data to the new format. We will cover this challenge in the Client-Side Data Migrations chapter.

Decide which features should work offline and which ones should not. Many teams miss this simple step that makes the planning of the offline functionality easier and avoids scope creep. I suggest starting with the key parts of the application and expanding this scope slowly. Get real-world feedback that the "main" offline mode works as expected. Can you leverage your approach in other parts of the app?

Decide how to handle offline edge cases. What do you want to do with extremely slow connections, where the phone is still online, but the data connection is overly slow? A robust solution is to treat this as offline and perhaps notify the user of this fact. What about timeouts? Will you retry?

Mobile devices going offline: An everyday scenario. How will you handle this?

Retries can be a tricky edge case. Say you have a connection that has not responded for some time — a soft timeout — and you retry another request. You might see race conditions or data issues if the first request returns, then the second request does too.

Synchronization of device and backend data is another common yet surprisingly challenging problem. This problem gets multiplied with multiple devices. You need to choose a conflict resolution protocol that works well enough for multiple parallel offline edits and is robust enough to handle connectivity dropping midway.

Retry strategies come with edge cases you need to think about. Before retrying, how can you be sure that the network is not down? How do you handle users frantically retrying and possibly creating multiple parallel requests? Will the app allow the same request to be made while the previous one has not completed? With a switch to offline mode, how can the app tell when the network has reliably recovered? How can the app differentiate between the backend service not responding or the network being slow? What about resource efficiency; should you look into using HTTP conditional requests with retries utilizing ETags or if-match headers?

With poor connectivity, the network request can sometimes time out. Sensible retry strategies or moving over to offline mode could be helpful. Both solutions come with plenty of tradeoffs to think about.

Many of the above situations can be solved relatively simply when using reactive libraries to handle network connections, such as RxSwift, Apple's Combine, RxJava or Kotlin Coroutines.

Requests that should not be retried come with a separate set of problems. For example, you might not want to retry a payment request while it is in progress. But what if it comes back as failed? You might think it is safe to retry. However, what if the request timed out, but the server made the payment? Then you will double charge the user.

As a consumer of backend endpoints, you should push all retries on API endpoints to be safe, by having these endpoints be idempotent. With idempotent endpoints, you have to obtain and send over idempotency keys and keep track of an additional state. You also have to worry about edge cases such as the app crashing and restarting and the idempotency key not being persisted. Implementing retries safely adds a lot of extra work for teams. You have to work closely with the backend team to map the use cases to design for.

As with state management, the key to a maintainable offline mode and weak connection support is simplicity. Use immutable states, straightforward sync strategies, and simple strategies to handle slow connections. Do plenty of testing with the right tools such as the Network Link Conditioner for iOS or the networkSpeed capability on Android emulators.

Resources for this chapter:
go.mobileatscale.com/7

8

ACCESSIBILITY

Accessibility is a big deal for popular applications, a few reasons:

1. If you have a large number of users, many of them will have various accessibility needs, finding it difficult or impossible to interact with your app without adequate support.
2. If the app is not accessible, there is an inherent legal risk for the app's publisher; several accessibility lawsuits targeting native mobile apps are already happening in the US.

Accessibility is not only a "nice" thing to do, your app quality increases as you make it more accessible. This thought comes from Victoria Gonda, who has collected excellent iOS and Android accessibility resources.

Before you start, you need to confirm the level of depth you will go into implementing the WCAG 2.1 mobile definitions. Ensuring the app is workable for sighted people over VoiceOver (iOS) / TalkBack (Android) and making sure colors/key elements contrast enough, are typical baseline expectations. Depending on your application type, you might need to consider hard of hearing people, or users with other accessibility needs.

Accessibility goes deeper than ensuring sighted people can use the app. Allowing accessibility preferences to work with the app, such as supporting the user's font size of choice — via Dynamic Type support on iOS and using scale-independent pixels as measurement on Android — are both practices you should follow. You also need to take device fragmentation into account. For example, in the Android world, OnePlus phone is known to have a different font size from the rest of the ecosystem.

Implementing accessibility from the start is a surprisingly low effort task on iOS and a sensible one for Android. Both platforms have thought deeply about accessibility needs and make it relatively painless to add accessibility features.

Retrofitting accessibility is where this problem can be time-consuming. Making accessibility part of the design process is a better way to go about things, which is why it is a good idea to make accessibility part of your planning/RFC process. Thinking about VoiceOver frames at a page level (iOS) and following accessibility best practices from the start are good investments.

Testing accessibility is something that needs planning. There are a few levels of accessibility testing you can and should add:

- **Automate** the parts of accessibility checks that can be automated, such as checking for accessibility labels on-screen elements. On iOS, you can also have VoiceOver content displayed as text and potentially automate these checks as well.
- **Manually test** accessibility features. Do this at least semi-regularly, as part of the release process.
- **Recruit accessibility users** in your beta program to get feedback directly from them. This is more feasible for

larger companies, but the payoff of having these users interact with the engineering team can be a major win.

- **Turn on accessibility features during development,** where it is sensible to do so. This way, you can inspect these working and get more empathy on how people who rely on these would use them.

Resources for this chapter:
go.mobileatscale.com/8

9

CI/CD & THE BUILD TRAIN

CI/CD for simple backend services and small web applications is straightforward. Yet, for even simple mobile applications, it is not. This is mostly because of the manual submission step of the app store. Doing a fully automated continuous deployment pipeline is impossible for iOS App Store apps, due to the manual review gate. On Android, you can automate this process, as you can with enterprise iOS apps.

Continuous deployment

App Store
Review Process

You cannot have a truly continuous deployment process to the App Store on iOS, thanks to the manual App Store Review process.

iOS and Android platforms are different; each requires its own build system and separate pipeline. When going with a third-party CI, it is worth choosing one who treats iOS and Android mobile builds as first-class, has a track record with mobile and can handle the scale your team or company wants. There are several vendors you can explore.

———

Bitrise is CI/CD built for mobile by mobile engineers. From pull request, to app store submission and beyond, Bitrise automates, monitors and improves your app development workflows. Teams who use Bitrise build better quality apps, deliver them faster, with developers who are happy.

Bitrise supports native Android, iOS, React Native, Flutter and builds with other popular mobile frameworks. Need support for a specific development step like testing, code signing, or notifying when a build has issues? With an open source library of hundreds of integrations you will probably find what you need, or be able to build it quickly.

More than 100,000 developers and thousands of organizations trust Bitrise. Try it for free at Bitrise.io and build better apps, faster.

———

Owning your own build infrastructure could give you more control and better experience than using cloud-based CI/CD vendors. Mobile engineering leaders at several engineering companies have noted they are happier having their build infrastructure in-house, even with the additional cost.

At a very large scale, you might decide to build in-house. At Uber, we did not have any vendor who could have reliably handled the number of builds we were doing, nor could they have provided the integration hooks our in-house system did.

You will probably find yourself using popular build tools to automate various build steps, such as uploading to the app store. For iOS, this will likely be Fastlane, and for Android builds running on Jenkins, it could be a Jenkinsfile or something similar.

Be wary of maintaining your homegrown CI system if you do not have dedicated people bandwidth to support this. I have seen startups repeatedly set up a Jenkins CI, get it running, only to realize months later that someone needed to keep dealing with infrastructure issues. I strongly suggest either to buy a vendor solution — and offload the infra part to the vendor — or to have a dedicated person or team own the build infrastructure for mobile.

For large companies, owning the build infrastructure might make sense. At Uber we had a dedicated mobile infra team who owned things like the iOS and Android monorepo or keeping master green, at scale. Other companies with large mobile teams and enough resources, also run their own CIs, using dedicated hardware. At the same time, companies like Rakuten have moved from an in-house CI setup to Bitrise, and are happy with the change.

The build train is the next step after you have a CI in place. A build train is a way to track the status of each of your weekly, or bi-weekly releases. Once a release cut is made for a "release candidate" for the app store, a series of validation steps need to happen; some of them automatic, some of them manual. These steps include running all automated tests, manual testing, localizing new resources, performance tests or a dogfooding or beta testing period.

Once the release candidate is validated, it is uploaded to the app store, and awaits approval. After approval, you might rollout a staged release, such as a phased rollout on iOS and staged rollouts on Android.

Your build train would visualize the status of all of the above; which commit was the build candidate cut, where the validation process is, and what the staged rollout status is. Build trains might be manually tracked by people owning the release process, and some companies with complicated release steps and mobile infra teams sometimes build their own homegrown solution.

Typical rollout stages include:

- **Dev/nightly build** of the app: A version of the app built by the CI/CD systems, sometimes done on a nightly cadence. Engineers or company employees are usually the only ones with access to this build.

- **Beta/dogfood release**: Usually released to most company employees and beta testers before staged rollout starts. A large enough beta group can help catch regressions and problems before general rollout.
- **General, staged rollout** in production. Rollout is often phased in production to a certain population percentage on Android.

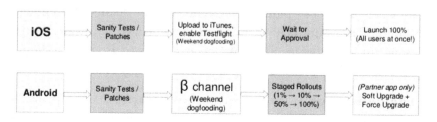

Steps for staged rollout for the Uber app

Whether to couple iOS and Android rollouts together, or do these separately, will be the choice of the release team. At Uber, we kept these coupled for the sake of simplicity and consistency. We had a weekly release cadence, and a more granular release schedule would have made little sense.

Mobile app release frequency will be down to what the team — or the company — decides to go with. Every mobile release adds testing overhead, which can be significant. At the same time, large releases with many new changes and features are more likely to have regressions, which in turn can further delay an already late release. Here are typical mobile release schedules which companies tend to adopt:

- **Weekly**: Large mobile teams with mature release and testing processes typically follow the approach of weekly build cuts. The build cut is then tested, and rolled out to beta users. When no regressions are found, the app makes it to the store, usually a week after the cut.

- **Every two weeks** Many companies choose this model to align with sprint lengths, and to reduce the overhead that comes with testing every release.
- **Less frequent or ad-hoc releases**: Small apps might release only when a significant enough change ships. This is a rare pattern for large or complex apps. Less frequent releases often relate to lower quality; more features shipped in one go, with more opportunities for regressions, which then take longer to fix. Consider increasing your shipping cadence to improve the quality of your app.

A non-representative poll on Twitter suggested that around 65% of 268 respondents released their mobile apps every two weeks or less.

How often do mobile engineering teams release apps? A poll.

The mobile build train is a way to visualize the status of all of the above; which commit was the build candidate cut, where the validation process is, and what the staged rollout status is. The release manager might manually track the build trains. Companies with complicated release steps and mobile infra teams tend to build their custom solution. We did this at Uber.

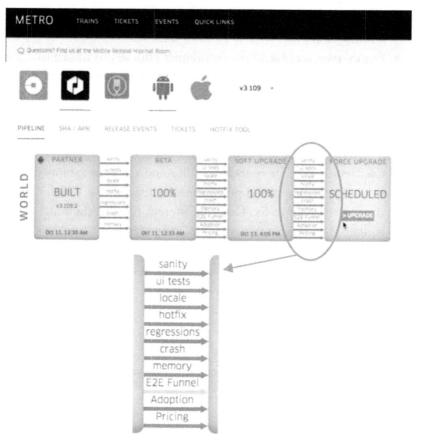

Uber's in-house build train system is called Metro. Between each release step, a series of manual or automated steps need to complete.

Define which checks need to complete before a release is "ready to go". Once you have these formalized, the more of the checks you can automate, the smoother the release process will be.

At Uber, the following tests needed to pass for each release phase:

- **UI tests** executing without failure. The UI tests suite was large enough that it did not make sense to run all tests on the CI. Before release, all tests were executed.
- **Manual sanity tests** executed by either teams owning these tests, or QA teams owning the process. The train

would not progress on failed sanity tests, or if tests were not executed.

- **Localization** completed for all strings. An automated check would inspect that there were no missing translations in the app.
- **Crash reports**. No regressions discovered during the beta testing process. Crashes during the beta phase would automatically trigger an alert or ticket and the team would need to investigate and resolve it, before rollout could continue.
- **Memory usage**. No regressions as per the memory profiling.
- **Business metrics**. No regressions during rollout ("E2E Funnel" metric). At Uber, we monitored request, dispatch and on-trip signals across regions. If a bug would cause a regression on any of these key metrics, we could detect the issue, and act to mitigate it.

Further reading:

- How mobile teams use release trains for increased speed and efficiency from Bitrise
- Keeping master green at scale from Uber
- The build and release process from Uber
- Create faster mobile release cycles from Lyft
- Release quality and mobile trains from SoundCloud
- Rapid releases at massive scale from Facebook
- The present and future of app release from Skyscanner
- Running own CI approaches from Mobile Native Foundation

Resources for this chapter:
go.mobileatscale.com/9

10

THIRD-PARTY LIBRARIES AND SDKS

As your app begins to grow and integrate with many third-party libraries, the build process becomes complex. Those libraries will have new versions, some of which are breaking changes that will require your source code to be updated correctly, and re-tested.

Third-party libraries can be a security liability. For example, new vulnerabilities are frequently discovered in the Google Play Core Library, allowing Local-Code-Execution (LCE). Users could be at risk of having their data stolen, or for their device to run unknown code when using apps with libraries that are exposed to LCE, especially if not updating to new app versions that address the security vulnerability.

You need to monitor for third-party library vulnerabilities on an ongoing basis. An option is to hire a third-party security provider to notify you when this happens.

Stability and reliability is another issue with third-party libraries. For example, in April 2020, the Google Maps SDK team pushed code to their backend that caused the apps embedding it to crash. This impacted hundreds of apps, including those for which Maps is a critical feature, causing these apps to lose money for the duration of the outage. In May 2020, something similar happened with the Facebook SDK, which had a repeat incident in July 2020.

This means that various companies had integrated the Google Maps SDK and the Facebook SDK to their apps, then built their binaries, and properly tested everything before pushing to the app stores. From the perspective of those companies, everything was under control. But those buggy changes from Google and Facebook were pushed to the backends of those SDKs, which is obviously not something that was testable when the integrations and builds were done. And once the crashes happened, there was nothing the developers of those apps could do. Their binaries were in the wild and they had no control.

This is why it is good practice to have a feature flag specifically for your third-party libraries, so that you can encapsulate the loading of those libraries and all the execution points, and easily disable any library via your backend, if there is a breaking change by the teams developing those SDKs.

Making third-party library updates reversible is difficult, and sometimes impossible to do. Major library updates can be risky. A pragmatic way to handle risky changes is rolling them out in a staged way, doing this using feature flags. However, it is usually close to impossible to ship an app with two library versions; even if you can embed two libraries, you would need dozens of feature flag touchpoints to cater for API changes.

Unfortunately, this means that library updates are one of the most risky changes in any app. You need to carefully test the app's behavior after the update, and to monitor crash reports and bug reports as the app progresses through the build train. It is good practice to do more employee testing and beta testing after major library updates than you would do with other, reversible changes.

There are many other risks that come with using third-party libraries that you want to consider. Several mobile teams create an evaluation criteria they run through before taking on a new third-party dependency. The list contains areas like these:

- **App size:** How much does the dependency add to the bundle size?
- **Tooling upgrade risks**: Could adding this dependency be a blocker when wanting to upgrade to a new XCode or Android Studio version?
- **Risk of no maintenance**: How likely is it that the dependency will not be maintained? For example, if a security vulnerability is discovered, can we reasonably expect the owner to resolve this in a short amount of time?
- **Third-party responsiveness**: How quickly does the owner respond to issues raised? Do they merge bug fixes in a timely manner?

It is a healthy approach to treat all third-party dependencies as risks, keep track of them, and re-evaluate the need to use them on a regular basis.

Resources for this chapter:
go.mobileatscale.com/10

11

DEVICE AND OS FRAGMENTATION

Device model and OS fragmentation is an everyday problem on both iOS and Android. Device fragmentation and weird, hardware-related bugs have always been familiar pain points on Android. OS fragmentation is less of an issue on iOS, while it keeps getting worse on Android.

Keeping on top of new OS releases and the accompanying API changes requires focus from mobile engineers. Both iOS and Android keep innovating; features and APIs keep being added, changed, and deprecated. It is not just big changes such as SwiftUI or Dark Mode on iOS 13, or biometric authentication APIs on iOS 8 (2014) and Android 10 (2019). There are several smaller APIs, such as credit card autofill on Android Oreo that exist on one platform, with no equivalent on the other. In all honesty, learning about the new APIs on WWDC or Google I/O and then adding them to the app, is the fun part.

Making sure the app keeps working without issues on older OS and devices is more of a challenge. You typically need to either set up an in-house device lab or use a third-party testing service to ensure that the app works correctly on all major models.

A peek into Facebook's device testing lab in 2016: the slatwall.

Android has far more quirks when it comes to edge cases and crashes that are specific to certain devices. For example, Samsung devices are well-known for strange crashes related to the Samsung Android customization, not to mention special layout considerations for the Galaxy Fold. Hardware drivers and GPS sensors can be a headache, including stack traces that are hard to make sense of.

Android has one more fragmentation issue; Android forks that do not run on Google's ecosystem. Apps built for Fire OS or future Huawei devices will not have access to Google Play Services. This means functionality like Firebase notifications will not work. Crash reports, user bug reports, and large-scale manual testing are ways you can stay on top of new issues and regressions. All of these are far more time-consuming and expensive than most people expect.

Deciding how and when to stop supporting old OS versions is a process your mobile team should put in, early on. The cost of supporting old iOS and Android versions is high and the payoff can be low. The business will naturally push to support as many devices as possible. The team needs to quantify what this

46

support adds up to. When revenue or profit from the old version is less than the cost to maintain, the pragmatic solution is to drop support for old OSes.

While there might be legal requirements in certain industries to support old OS versions, the fewer versions you support, the faster you are able to move. As of 2021, it is common for Android teams to support from version 24 and up (Nougat) - but rarely going back to before v21 (Lollipop). On iOS, thanks to more rapid OS adoption, many businesses drop support for versions beyond the last two or three, soon after a new OS release.

Resources for this chapter:
go.mobileatscale.com/11

12

IN-APP PURCHASES

In-app purchases (IAP) are unique to iOS and Android in the amount of revenue they can drive, and the challenge of testing these on large and complex apps.

IAP is unique to mobile platforms and when you sell digital products, not implementing it is rarely an option. You have to pay a hefty fee of 15% on revenue up to $1 million annually (both for iOS and for Android), and 30% above this. On top of the cut, you still have to work your way through numerous limitations and frustrations.

———

RevenueCat makes it easy to build and manage iOS and Android in-app purchases at scale. With a few lines of code RevenueCat provides IAP infrastructure, customer analytics, data integrations, and gives you time back from dealing with edge cases and updates across the platforms.

Created by developers, for developers, thousands of the world's best apps use RevenueCat to power their in-app purchases and subscriptions. Get started for free at RevenueCat.com.

———

The biggest limitations of IAP you are likely to come across are these:

- **Different iOS, Android IAP models and capabilities** and likely a different model from a web product. For example, Google Play allows pausing of subscriptions to prevent voluntary churn, but iOS does not. This is one of the several differences between the two platforms.
- **Implementing IAP state changes to happen** in a bullet-proof way. Customers will expect IAP effects to happen immediately. However, doing so might be more of a challenge. You could do a purely client-side implementation which can be simpler to implement, but that makes the subscription fully tied to the App Store account. It also opens up attack vectors for bad actors, such as setting back the device clock, or running a modified version of your app that "unlocks" IAP functionality. You could wait on backend callbacks, but this can mean delays, and having to deal with more edge cases. These edge cases will be unique to your app and your IAP functionality.
- **Rigid pricing**. With Apple, you can only choose from predefined price tiers, and changing the pricing for subscriptions becomes complex. You will find it challenging to set prices per country if your pricing is different from the suggested guidelines. If you decide to implement IAP as a purely client-side approach, you will also have to hardcode your products in the binary.
- **Poor API documentation.** The subscription APIs for iOS are under-documented. You will find yourself troubleshooting how certain aspects of this works. Android IAP APIs are better documented and you will have less trouble with them.
- **Reporting challenges**. Answering the question of "how

much revenue does a specific user generate for us" becomes unexpectedly challenging, if not practically impossible. The challenge is calculating the net proceeds from the gross purchases a user makes, including the proceeds from follow-up transactions. A common approach is saving the gross price information, and making estimates of net revenue from various data points such as gross prices, aggregated daily reports and the App Store pricing matrix.

- **Accounting, reconciliation and tax woes.** Both iOS and Android do payouts differently and report/handle taxes differently. Apple's fiscal calendar is crazy by itself, including a 35-day accounting month. Your accounting team will be pulling their hair trying to work their way through how things work, and someone from the mobile team will likely need to help them figure out how the numbers add up.

- **Subscriptions support**. On iOS, you do not have the tooling to cancel or refund a subscription, even if the user asks you to do this. See the subscriptions page for Disney+ for an example of the type of awkward customer messaging this results in.

- **Mapping IAP users to your backend systems**. You need to pair App Store user credentials to the metadata you store in your systems. If you fail to do so, you might have to display errors that confuse users and require assistance from customer support.

- **Restoring IAPs flow**. What should happen when a customer buys and sets up a new phone? Things should "just work". To make this happen, you might need to add additional business logic to this flow. Apple has a good overview on steps you might need to take. A note for iOS: transaction IDs can change when restoring a receipt, which is something you need to handle on the backend.

- **IAP endpoints availability** is not at 100%. For example, Apple's verifyreceipt endpoint has been known to return 5xx responses, obscure error messages or incorrect data. Apple will rarely communicate outages, so many engineers rely on third-party monitoring such as Downdetector.

- **IAPs on non-Google Play stores** such as Amazon or Huawei is an additional challenge. You need to consult the respective developer documentation. You need to balance the cost of building and supporting IAPs on these platforms with the revenue these platforms will generate.

- **B2B use cases** and supporting volume discounts, or providing VAT receipts. While Apple does have a volume purchase program for apps, there is nothing similar for IAP. For VAT invoices, you need to direct users to find this option in the App Store, or request this via Google Play.

IAP edge cases and handling them should give you plenty of work. Most of these edge cases are not unique to IAP, but will be challenges on the web as well. You still need to validate these cases.

- **IAP states** and handling them, such as cancelling a one-off purchase, cancelling a subscription or re-purchasing after cancelling.

- **Grace periods and trials** for subscriptions. Can people extend their trial, if they need more time?

- **Upgrading, downgrading, changing** subscriptions. The more tiers you have, the more edge cases to think about.

- **Discounts** and working with these. You have to use promotional offers or subscription offers on iOS and promo codes on Android. Managing, keeping track and retiring discounts gets more difficult with each new one.

- **Your IAP backend endpoints going down.** If your IAP solution relies upon the App Store Server Notifications, or the Google Play real-time developer notifications for server-to-server events, you want to have close to 100% availability for *persisting* these events, even if your processing capability is down. The App Store might retry if your endpoint is not available, but this behavior is not documented for iOS, nor for Android.

- **Other edge cases** such as refunds, credit card failures, account hold, grace period or paused subscriptions on Android.

Manually testing that in-app purchases work is a smaller challenge itself. Both Apple and Google provide ways to test IAPs; Apple offers their Sandbox on iOS and StorekitTest for unit testing. For Android, on Google Play you can test with license testers in the Play Store sandbox.

Note that the sandbox environment comes with limitations. There will be some real-world scenarios you cannot replicate in this setting. You will probably also have to tweak your backend to allow for sandbox testing.

Testing for various IAP scenarios is where validating in-app-purchase functionality can become complex.

- **One-off purchase testing** is the most straightforward scenario. Still, you want to test for all purchase types to ensure they work.
- **Validating receipts content** is an often overlooked step. The information on the customer receipt should be clear, in order to avoid unwarranted chargebacks or complaints.
- **Subscriptions upgrade** testing means both testing for people upgrading from no subscription to a subscription tier and ensuring all subscription tiers work as expected.
- **Subscription upgrades and downgrades** are things you should test for. Scenarios can especially be tricky when downgrading. Are there scenarios you need to pay attention to, where subscribers could lose some of the data they entered?
- **Subscriptions changed outside the app.** Customers can upgrade or downgrade subscriptions while the app is closed, or in the background. You need to handle these

cases separately, making sure the app "reacts" to these changes when started, or resumed.

- **Crossgrade between subscriptions** is a more rare case. However, if you have multiple subscription tiers that are not on an upgrade or downgrade path, for example, switching between a monthly and a yearly subscription, then you need to test for these cases.
- **Subscription changes and grace periods** being in place is particularly tricky to test because these grace periods are usually days or weeks. You do want to ensure the grace periods are handled correctly.
- **Documenting** test steps, expected outcomes, accounts to test with and other information needed to execute the tests.
- **Staged testing**. You need to detect and parse the environment field in the webhook requests for IAP to differentiate between sandbox, and production callbacks.

Apple has a comprehensive overview of test scenarios you might want to test for and from which to take inspiration for Android.

Automating IAP testing is challenging, both due to the limited tooling available, and the complexity of manually testing IAPs. Automating should be a step easier if you have a well-documented manual testing process for IAP. Tools that you could use for IAP automation include StoreKit Test (iOS) or tools such as BrowserStack.

Customer support is critical to ensure your customer service team has a good connection to engineers owning IAP so you can spot and act on IAP issues. This is especially true if IAPs makes up the majority of your app revenue.

You will eventually want to help put runbooks in place for the customer support team. How should they handle common complaints? How should they go about appeasing customers who have valid complaints? What if customers report a new bug that the team is working on fixing? Much of these questions exist outside of the engineering decision bubble. Still, I suggest engineering has a seat at the table where these discussions take place.

At the very least, engineers should have visibility on customer feedback; app store ratings, customer messages, and have the ability to deepdive into common issues around the IAP functionality. Customers who pay should rightfully expect things "to just work" and as engineers, we should know when and why this is not the case.

Multi-platform IAP challenges will be a recurring theme you need to deal with, assuming you sell across iOS, Android and possibly other platforms such as the web. Each platform will have different tax policies. You have to deal with a customer buying the IAP on one platform, then switching over to another one.

For example, what would happen when a user buys an IAP on iOS, and then buys a new Android phone; would they subscribe again? Would you build a flow to support "transferring" the subscription? Would your backend "detect" the same person subscribing on two platforms? Would you have a customer support runbook about what to advise people who are about to change phones? What does your competition do in this case; and can you do better?

A/B testing IAPs is challenging, to say the least: neither Apple nor Google have native support for this approach. You will have to come up with your own solutions to experiment with pricing points and will most likely find yourself setting up and having to maintain separate subscription groups. Customers will be "locked in" to these groups after the test, adding an "IAP debt" you need to manage.

Locking in customers to the same subscription group has financial incentives. If a customer is subscribed for more than a year, Apple's subscription revenue cut drops from 30% to 15%. However, if users move to a different group, this timer "resets". This means there is little financial incentive to create too many of these groups.

Experimenting with different "packaging" such as tiers, feature sets and pricing, becomes even more challenging with IAP, compared to the web. A common challenge is testing different sets of pricing with different groups in your user base. You need to plan well ahead if you want to try anything beyond a simple subscription offering.

Grandfathered subscription pricing is another problem you could face, especially when you are selling a SaaS offering through your app. Let's say that you try out a package that does not work well with most users, and you retire this offering. It is an expected best practice that you grandfather customers who bought this package and support this retired offering for some time. You face both churn and user backlash if you do not and your brand will also suffer.

A common and sensible approach to experimenting with different IAP subscriptions is this.

1. Plan ahead to have clear next steps, both for when the pricing experiment is successful, and when it is not. What are your success metrics?
2. Run the experiment for a short time period.
3. Offer a one-month, cancellable subscription with the pricing experiment.
4. If the pricing experiment does not work out and you need to up prices, be as flexible as you can with customers who subscribed for this pricing plan.

The lack of IAP tooling support for any non-basic scenario is what will likely cause you the most headaches. Neither Apple, nor Google have built anything beyond a simple one-off or a subscription product. When you are building complex apps, or apps with many users, you will likely find the business wanting more options, and yourself looking at how to work around a limiting IAP feature set.

———

In-App Purchases: The Biggest Challenges

Andy Boedo, software engineer at RevenueCat shares some of the biggest IAP challenges he has observed while working at Elevate Labs and RevenueCat.

Supporting both iOS and Android IAPs

If you intend to support both iOS and Android, you have to implement and maintain the code for handling IAPs on both, which is tough in itself. Then, you have to track and match purchases for users on both sides, so that if a user buys an item on Android, they can access the same item on iOS. This is a pain point that RevenueCat can help with.

IAP Testing

There has been great progress with tools to test IAP, such as StoreKit Test. However, there is still much testing that is impossible to do with sandbox environments. For example, you cannot test iOS Family Sharing Subscriptions, different storefronts, non-renewing subscriptions and other use cases.

To do proper testing, you want to use physical devices. With Apple, this means having several physical devices, because watchOS, tvOS, macOS, macCatalyst and iOS all support purchases, but features vary by OS and version. For thorough testing, you need lots of devices, all running different OS versions. For Android, physical testing multiples by the number of supported Android devices and versions.

Client-side IAPs Challenges

A purely client-side IAP implementation will not consider some edge cases. Going with an on-device validation approach will still mean seeing load times, as you need to refresh the receipt from Apple. The on-device validation approach is also not resistant to device clock changes.

When going with a client-side IAP implementation, the app needs to know the product identifiers (strings) that will be offered to the user. When going with a purely client-side approach the products need to be hardcoded. This means you cannot update products and pricing unless you update the app. A reason to go with a backend-driven IAP purchase is so you can control the products you offer from your service, and avoid them being hardcoded.

Finally, you might need to embed Apple's public key in the app in order to verify receipt signature. If this public key changes, you need to update it in the app. You also need to implement the validation logic.

Limited Subscriptions Tooling

Most customers will assume that you have control over cancelling and refunding subscriptions, and assume you are intentionally not granting them a refund. The reality is that even if you want to, you do not have the tooling to make changes to subscriptions. Unless you are clear in setting expectations, this confusion can be a common source of one-star reviews.

———

Collaborating with the backend team which captures IAP user data will be critical in building a solid product. The backend team will likely have to work with an iOS, Android and possibly a web team because of each platform handling payments and subscriptions in a different way.

It will be down to you to educate the backend team on how iOS or Android handles IAP, and what edge cases you need to test. Working with the backend team is also a good opportunity to get exposed to how IAP works on the other platform, and how the web handles the same problem space.

Further reading:

- Testing in-app purchases with sandbox on iOS and Android from RevenueCat
- Testing in-app purchases with Sandbox from Apple
- The guide to iOS subscription testing from RevenueCat
- Testing your Google Play billing library integration from Google
- Testing purchases in Google Play Store Sandbox from RevenueCat
- In-app purchases on iOS from Ray Wenderlich
- Testing in-app purchases on Android
- iOS in-app purchase and testing
- Testing in-app purchases in iOS 14

Resources for this chapter:
go.mobileatscale.com/12

Basic idea here:
in app purchases
are a pain
in the ass

PART II

CHALLENGES DUE TO APP COMPLEXITY

Things start to get interesting as an app grows. You keep adding new features to the app, while also tweaking the existing ones. Soon, the app that used to be a few screens gets so complex that, if you were to print out screens on a navigation flow chart, it would cover the whole wall.

When working with a large and complex app, you do run into additional challenges. How do you deal with increasingly complicated navigation patterns? What about non-deterministic event combinations? How do you localize across several languages, and how do you scale your automated and manual tests?

Let's jump in.

13

NAVIGATION ARCHITECTURE WITHIN LARGE APPS

Navigation within mobile apps is just as much of an underrated problem area as deeplink challenges. When the app is small, we tend not to pay much attention to it. As the app grows, we realize the navigation architecture has become a beast that needs to be tamed, as the number of screens and transitions grows.

While both iOS and Android provide basic navigation concepts, they leave defining of the navigation architecture up to engineers. In turn, we tend to reinvent the wheel on navigation. This is mostly out of necessity, as neither iOS or Android ship with navigation approaches that scale well beyond simple apps.

Having a well-defined app navigation strategy with good separation of app state is key for any decent-sized app. What navigation happens between screens and components? What triggers this animation between taps and gestures? Is navigation independent of app state?

separate nav from app state [handwritten margin note]

Many teams only build this map once they code themselves in a corner, discovering they have built inconsistent navigation solutions that lead to bugs when the user gets in unexpected states.

Inconsistent navigation can be as visible as the app using popups, toasts, full-screen modals, or screens inconsistently. It can mean that different animations are used between different screens. It usually also means lots of code duplication in instructing the app to navigate.

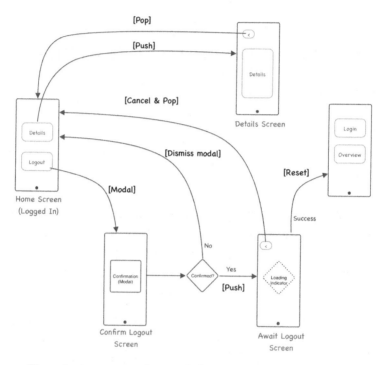

The navigation structure of an app. Is the navigation structure the same for your apps across iOS and Android?

Asynchronous navigation is a common issue that few engineers consider handing ahead of time. By asynchronous navigation, I mean when something needs to finish before navigation can continue. Logging into the application or submitting a form are examples of this. What happens when the user attempts to navigate away during this phase? If you do not plan and test for this scenario, the app can get into strange states. When using RIBs, workflows provide an elegant solution to this problem.

A navigation framework or consistent navigation approach is something you will find yourself either building, enforcing, or utilizing an existing component for, with more complex apps.

On iOS, there is no one native navigation component you can use. While several open source projects provide help, navigation is far from a solved problem on this platform. As John Sundell concludes in the article, *Navigation in Swift*: "having a nice way to perform navigation, in a way that doesn't paint you into corners, can be really tricky."

Android is perhaps a step ahead. The Jetpack Navigation Architecture Component is becoming the preferred out-of-the-box library for navigation. It works well enough, except for lack of support for some edge cases. Jetpack was released in 2018. Apps that build their own solutions on top of Activities and Fragments and often need to decide if they maintain their own stack, or migrate over. Even without Jetpack, Android is more opinionated in its navigation approach, like guidelines on the Up and Back keys and having a back stack in place.

Mobile and tablet navigation differences is an interesting edge case. If your app has larger screens and forms, mobile devices might have multiple steps or screens, while the tablet version uses a single one. This scenario is more likely with iOS, where both the phone and the tablet sizes are well-defined. Supporting this scenario is not too difficult, but only if you plan for it.

Resources for this chapter:
go.mobileatscale.com/13

14

APPLICATION STATE & EVENT-DRIVEN CHANGES

What drives changes in the UI of your mobile app? It could be users tapping on certain parts of it, data arriving from the backend, or perhaps a timing function. Most of the changes are driven by events, as we discussed in the State Management chapter.

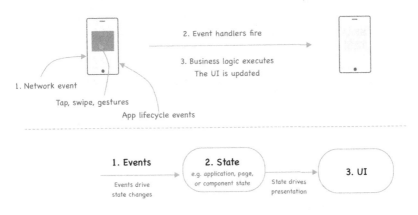

Events driving state changes in mobile apps

As the app grows in complexity, so does the number of possible states. Some state changes might trigger other state changes. For example, a component changing its state after a user tap might trigger the state of the page, or application, to change.

Mobile apps typically have more states than web or thick client apps. This is due to the variety of lifecycle events they need to support, such as app locking, app switching, and background mode, not to mention offline mode support adding several other states. Web apps have fewer lifecycle events and seldom support offline mode extensively, while thick client apps have fewer lifecycle events, and connectivity drops are much more of a rarity than with mobile.

The larger and more complex the app, the more likely bugs are caused by a combination of events that are out of the ordinary. The problem with out of the ordinary events is they are difficult to plan or test for. For example, a background push notification that causes a state change in a component might arrive right after the user locks the screen of the app, causing a different state change. One of the more rare inbound events might be consumed by independent components / teams, and this combination results in exotic bugs.

Follow state management best practices to keep the number of bugs low that happen because of state change issues. Keep state as immutable as possible and store models as immutable objects that emit state changes.

Record invalid states with information to replay or debug, so you have details on what went wrong and how to reproduce the issue. Using a bug reporting vendor tool is the easiest way to start and there are plenty to choose from. Several crash reporting tools also come with a bug reporting component.

Typically, the bug reporting tool would be shown to beta users to submit issues. When submitting the bug report, you'll also need to include the series of events that happened leading up to the issue and enough information so that you can debug what happened. Most bug reporting tools will allow you to attach the logs emitted during the session Your challenge will be to emit enough logs to make bug reproduction possible.

Automatically replay, pause, rewind, and debug the user's session; this is what an ideal tool to debug application state issues would do. You want to have a log, not just of user events, but of incoming network notifications. Being able to do this on a per-thread basis is important in order to debug cross-thread issues. While there are such session replay tools on the web; unfortunately, on iOS and Android, we are left with either having to build custom tools to do the above, or to work with debug logs and memory dumps for the foreseeable future.

15

LOCALIZATION

Both iOS and Android offer opinionated ways to implement localization. iOS supports exporting localizations for translation, while
Android builds on top of resource strings. The tooling is slightly
different, but the concept is similar. To localize your app and define
the strings, you want to localize and ship the localized strings as a
separate resource in the binary. Still, with large apps and many
locales, you quickly run into challenges with this workflow.

**Deciding what to localize in the app versus doing so on
the backend** is one of the first challenges any growing app will
face. By using the "default" iOS and Android localization approach,
resources you localize within the app will be "stuck" with the binary:
you cannot change phrases or update mistakes. If you implement
serving localized strings from a vendor solution, or your backend,
you have more flexibility in this regard and you only need to do one
localization pass for both iOS and Android.

The topic of how "smart" the mobile app should be and what
strings should live here, versus just getting them from the backend,
runs deeper. We will go into more detail in Part 3: Backend-driven
mobile apps. The more localization the backend does, the better.

Ado it on the
BE

Backend-heavy localization keeps client-side logic low and reduces the number of resources for localization on mobile. While delegating more localization to the backend usually needs work, both on the iOS and Android app workflows, it leads to easier maintainability in the long run.

When supporting a large number of locales, you need to ensure that all localization translations are complete before shipping to the app store. You might be using third-party localization services or an in-house team to do so. Assuming you have a build train, you want to allow the train to proceed only after all new resources have been localized.

Ensuring iOS and Android use the same language and localization is yet another challenge. Especially for larger brands, it is important that both the iOS and Android apps use the same — or at least similar — languages. A consistent language is not only beneficial for the brand, it also helps customer support handle issues reported by users. It is hard to ensure this consistency without some shared localization tooling or the iOS and Android teams working closely with each other. Having the same designer and PM overseeing both apps also helps. Using the same localization IDs or keys is a good way to reduce duplication and this needs to be done through the iOS and Android teams agreeing on conventions.

At Uber, we used an in-house localization tool across iOS, Android, backend, and web. This tool was integrated to generate iOS and Android resources and to track the completeness of localization. Was it overkill to build a dedicated tool just for localization? For Uber's sophisticated use cases years back, I do not think so. Back then, there were few to no good localization tools across all stacks.

The space has changed since, though, and there are many localization vendors in the mobile space. Before building your own, it is worth seeing if you can find one that fits your needs.

Localized custom fonts is a frequently overlooked area. It is common for larger companies and those with strong brand identities to use custom fonts. However, this custom font does not always support every glyph for an app's supported set of languages.

It is tricky enough to confirm which languages and characters your custom font is missing support for. This is even more of an issue when using these fonts to display user-generated content, as you do not have control over this input. Once you have figured out your use cases and edge cases, you either need to have this support added or — more frequently, — use a different font for unsupported locales. It gets even more difficult to manage a consistent, cross-platform mapping of fonts and languages, based on which languages each font supports.

When using custom fonts, you need to include these in the binary, adding to the app's size. We will discuss app size in more detail in Part 3 of the series.

Currencies formatted differently on iOS and Android on certain locales is another pain point that multi-language, multi-platform apps displaying monetary values encounter. Web has a similar problem with the inconsistency; Indian rupee values are a good example of this. The problem is especially pronounced when using currency types to add or subtract values. A possible work-around is for the backend to format all currency data to the locale, and the client not doing any math operations, or formatting currency strings.

Date and time formatting will have similar challenges to currencies. Different countries and regions will display dates and times in various ways. You need to make sure the app accounts for this.

Supporting right-to-left (RTL) languages can often go beyond just translations. Most people reading this book will either be used to LTR and Latin-based languages or speak it fluently enough. However, when designing UIs for RTL languages like Arabic, Hebrew, and others, it is not just strings that need to be mirrored; the layout of the app might need to be changed. "Mirroring" the layout is a common approach, but it might result in strange UIs for native speakers and users. It is best to have locals involved in this process, both for development and for testing.

Unique locales are always worth additional attention. In my experience, Japanese and German are locales are worthy of even more checks because they can both be more verbose than English, and you want to make sure the layouts, paddings, and line breaks still work for these locales.

The Skyscanner app with English, Japanese and German languages. German is often a good choice to stress test the app, as the language is more verbose.

Testing localization is no small effort. In an ideal world, a native speaker would go through every flow of your app after each localization change. In reality, this rarely happens because it is too expensive to do. Most large companies rely on beta testers using the app with different locales to report glaring inconsistencies. For example, at Uber, we could rely on this method to spot localization issues early. Thousands of Uber employees dogfooded the app every week, alongside beta testers. Localization issues almost always got caught before the app got pushed to the app store.

You might need to define a workflow to validate localization changes. What should happen when a localized string changes in the app? Should this trigger an action to manually inspect the change? Should developers for the screen be notified? Should the release manager ship a new version of the app, even if there are no other changes? These might seem like minor questions. They are not. They are especially not when people translating strings work independently to engineers writing the code. Someone needs to define a workflow of not just adding, but updating and testing localization.

Snapshot testing is an underrated testing tool for localization. With snapshot tests, you can quickly and easily generate snapshots for screens in any locale, or even with pseudo-localization. Engineers can then spot layout issues much faster, and have reference images showcasing the issues. On top of helping engineers, you can share the snapshot test screenshots with people doing the translation, so they get additional context on how the translated text will appear.

Pseudo-localization is a smart way to test localization working, without going through the localization exercise. It means replacing all localizable elements with a pseudo-language that is readable by developers, but which contains most of the "tricky" elements of other languages, such as special characters or longer strings.

For example, a pseudo-localized version of "Find Help" could appear as "[ʃﬁﬁñðððð Ĥééééélþ]. Microsoft used this approach while developing Windows Vista and Netflix uses this approach for their product development cycle. Shopify built a ruby tool to generate strings like this, and you can find an npm package that was inspired by the approach at Netflix.

Phrases that should not be localized are one final edge case. At Uber, we decided not to localize certain brand terms like Uber Cash or Uber Wallet. Some teams were not aware of this request and went ahead and translated the strings in certain screens, meaning the owning teams had to test on all locales to find these issues. Several testers also reported the lack of these translations on a regular basis. This was a bit of noise we had to manage.

There are plenty of vendors who can help with mobile localization. Localization is rarely done in isolation only on iOS and Android; it is more commonly done as a whole, including the web, emails and other customer-facing properties. Localization vendors include POEditor, Loco, Transifex, Crowdin, Phrase, Lokalise, OneSky, Wordbee, Text United, and several others.

Further reading:

- Pseudo-localization from Netflix
- Why you should care about pseudo-localization from Shopify
- Design for internationalization from Dropbox
- Practical internationalization tips from Shopify
- Localizing across multiple platforms from Slack
- Localizing native apps with Localicious from Picnic
- Android localization guide from ProAndroidDev
- Using adaptive width strings for iOS localization from Daniel Martín

Resources for this chapter:
go.mobileatscale.com/15

16

MODULAR ARCHITECTURE & DEPENDENCY INJECTION

As apps become large, it often makes sense to build parts of the application as reusable components or modules. For large companies, either with several apps or several mobile teams, reusing the code owned by another team becomes a no-brainer. For example, a mobile platform team might own networking and shared architecture components. A Money team would build and own payments components — this was my team at Uber! — and a Maps team would own all things mapping-related. Components and modules in the app would often map to the structure of the company's teams, mirroring the observation known as Conway's law.

With multiple modules, modules need to have a way to define their dependencies, both at a module and a class level. This concept is dependency injection, a form of inversion of control. It is a simple, yet often underrated concept in mobile development and one that is far more commonplace with backend and web projects.

A major challenge with dependency injection is the amount of work it takes to modify or update dependencies if you do not use a framework to solve this. Even without using a framework, the time-consuming nature of this is a trade-off for clearer abstractions and good testability.

Dependency injection is a powerful tool for maintaining testable code consistently across the codebase. With dependency injection, classes that have multiple dependencies can be unit-tested by passing mock dependency classes when instantiating them. Larger, modular apps tend to introduce this concept one way or the other.

Manual dependency injection — creating all interfaces, then hard-coding all dependencies — works fine when there are few such dependencies. However, as the number of components and the number of dependencies grow, maintaining and updating dependencies becomes more difficult. Spotting things such as circular dependencies also becomes tricky and using dependency injection frameworks begins to make more sense.

Android has a mature dependency injection framework that analyzes dependencies' compile-time, called Dagger2. Google recently introduced Hilt on Dagger; a dependency framework built on top of Dagger, and Koin is becoming more popular with Kotlin.

On iOS, there have historically not been similar frameworks. At Uber, we built, used, and open-sourced Needle, based on similar concepts. We would have had trouble scaling the code with over a hundred engineers working on the same codebase without dependency injection. We used this tool to be explicit about all class dependencies, make unit testing easy — and non-negotiable for most of the code — and reuse components across teams.

Resources for this chapter:
go.mobileatscale.com/16

17

AUTOMATED TESTING

If you are not doing a decent level of automated testing on a large app, then you are digging a hole for yourself. By a large app, I mean either a complex codebase or a large number of people contributing to it.

The different types of automated test for mobile are these:

- **Unit test**: the simplest of all automated tests, testing an isolated component, also called the "unit." For iOS and Android, this would usually mean testing the behavior of a method on a class, or a specific behavior of a class. These tests are simple to write and understand and are fast to run.
- **Integration tests** are a step up in complexity from unit tests. They test the behavior of multiple "units" interacting. These tests are more complex and take longer to run than unit tests. They might or might not use mocks. Here is a good overview of mobile integration testing from John Sundell.
- **Snapshot test:** one comparing the layout of a UI element or page to a reference image. It is a cheap and fast way to ensure code changes do not result in unexpected UI

changes. Popular snapshot testing frameworks include iOSSnapshotTestCase, SwiftSnapshotTesting, and Screenshot Tests for Android.

- **UI test**: a test that exercises the UI, and tests for the UI behaving in a specific way. Inputs come through UI automation, and the UI is inspected to validate assumptions. UI tests are usually the most complex ones to write and take the longest time to run. UI tests might have their data layer — the backend endpoints — mocked.

Unit testing is a baseline tool for sustainable engineering, assuming you have a team of more than a few engineers and a mobile app that is considered complex. Unit testing business logic, paired with code reviews, reduces bug rate, keeps the code cleaner, and increases knowledge sharing within the team. It also is the safety net for making meaningful refactors and to be able to keep cleaning up tech debt. Unit testing comes with a pyramid of benefits. I write about these compounding benefits in more detail in the article The Pyramid of Unit Testing Benefits.

When you inherit an application that has few tests in-place, and the parts of the app were not built in a testable manner, you often have little choice but to add integration tests and to slowly add unit tests for the new pieces of code. Retrofitting the existing parts of the application might make little sense.

Integration testing is more complex than unit tests. You test how two or more classes, modules, or other units work together. The most common case for integration tests is ensuring that library integrations work as expected. Integration testing is especially useful for libraries and modules you write that other app parts will reuse. The integration test would exercise the public API of the library / module and confirm the component works as expected.

A special case of integration tests is UI testing parts of the app, but not doing this end-to-end. For example, testing that a button click navigates to a specific screen (iOS) / activity (Android) would be an integration test.

Integration tests are more expensive to write and maintain than unit tests, though they can also be more valuable, given they test a larger surface area. There is no golden rule on whether you should lean on these or unit tests more. It all depends on your environment and project.

Snapshot tests are the next line of automated testing. They are a special form of integration or UI/end-to-end test. A page is spun up, a screenshot taken and compared to a stored image. The data used is usually mocked. If it is different, the test fails, attaching the new image as the reason for failure.

Snapshot tests are cheap to build, and can help with faster iteration cycles for engineers. After you change something in the UI, you rerun the tests, and compare the results to what the changed UI now looks like.

At Uber, we took over iOSSnapshotTestCase from Facebook and used this tool heavily, but only on iOS. Back then, the Android team decided not to have snapshot tests as they felt the effort to do "proper" snapshot testing would have been too high on this platform, thanks to the variety of Android device sizes.

If the reference images for snapshot tests are stored in the repo, this can become a problem as there are more such tests. With thousands of test cases, these images take up lots of space which slows repo checkouts and updates. At Uber, we ended up moving snapshot images out of the repo, creating a CI job that tracked changes to the snapshots, as PRs are merged on main. The CI creates a task if changes are detected. If the change is expected, developers can just close the ticket. If not, they can create a follow-up diff to resolve the issue. This approach involved building custom tooling, working around the references images not being checked into the repo.

While snapshot testing is increasingly being adopted by a variety of apps and teams, it is not a one-size fits all tool. Much of the usefulness of these tests will depend on your app. Covering the "core" flows that you do not want to change without noticing, is a good start to these tests.

Automated UI testing is where native mobile tooling gets quite limiting when done at scale. Apple provides UI testing out of the box, which is a manual process to record, then replay. This tool works fine for a few test cases. For larger apps, you have to engineer a more robust solution and use approaches such as robots or page objects. Capital One showcases a nice reference implementation for robot pattern testing and Wantedly shared a good reference for the page object pattern approach. Building your own system using robots or page objects is not too difficult and scales pretty well.

Android natively supports UI testing with Espresso and with the UI Automator test frameworks. These are both powerful solutions that scale well for larger apps.

Once you hit dozens or more test cases, the existing tooling will feel somewhat limited. For one, none of these test frameworks support mocking of network responses and you have to use other tools like Mocker on iOS or using OkHttp's MockWebServer functionality on Android. You must choose a mocking approach and decide how to manage the mock test data.

Any team that writes more than 20-30 UI tests will run into the problem of how long these tests take to run. And the dilemma of whether to execute these tests before merging to master, or just occasionally. This issue highlights two things:

- **Consider where you focus your testing efforts** in the context of the testing pyramid. Yes, UI tests are important, but they are the most expensive ones to write and maintain and the slowest to run. Do you have the right level of investment in the other tests?
- **Solving for running UI tests at scale** has many benefits. Engineers do not have to overthink adding new UI tests and can do so confidently. The talk, Two Years of UI testing, outlines a few possible solutions for doing so. At Uber, we spent considerable time and effort to parallelize UI test execution, detect flakey tests, and to track / report the cost and benefits of UI tests.

Mocked live data for testing is another complexity of automated testing and using mocked data has several advantages:

- **Speed**. Tests run faster when mocking data upfront, as opposed to fetching it live. Live data needs to go through the network.
- **Edge cases**. It is much easier to set up mock data that represents edge case scenarios, than doing this with live data.
- **Reliability**. When using live data, the test can fail due to network or backend problems. While this might be a good thing in some cases — especially if the backend should be up all of the time — it can also generate noise.
- **Frequency**. When tests are fast, it makes sense to run them on every change. Run tests locally which exercise the code that was changed. This means close to immediate feedback to engineers. When tests are slower, they will typically only be run pre-merge. The feedback loop gets longer, making development loops also longer.

Using mocked data comes with some problems you need to address, especially as the number of test cases grows:

- **Live data and mock data being out of sync**. Testing is not worth much if the tests pass, but the app fails. You want to somehow detect when the live data changes, and you need to update your mocks. This is easier said than done.
- **Test data management.** As soon as you have many tests using mocked data, you want to come up with a structured way to both store this data, and to label the use cases they support. There's no definite solution. Some teams keep the data in the code, some use human-readable formats like JSON, and others keep this data in a file hierarchy. Choose a solution that will make both understanding and modifying the test data easy, while not

making it too difficult to add new mock data and test cases.

- **Dynamic data experiences**. With more complex UI tests, you often want to set up a scenario where the data changes dynamically. For example, you might want to simulate a user with a set of attributes, then reset the app and simulate with another set of attributes. This case is an extension of how you manage test data. As your number of scenarios increases, keeping both the data and the tests easy to maintain becomes more tricky.

Testing strategies vary greatly between companies and teams. Each group will have different constraints and goals, and will utilize different types of tests to make this happen. As inspiration, here are a few numbers on how certain companies approach testing as of 2021, based on this Mobile Native Foundation discussion:

- Spotify had ~32,000 unit and integration tests, ~1,600 snapshot tests and ~500 UI tests.
- Airbnb had ~10,000 unit tests and ~30,000 screenshot tests.
- Robinhood had thousands of unit tests, ~400 snapshot tests and ~15 blocking E2E tests.
- Nordstrom had ~29,800 unit tests, ~1,500 UI tests and a handful of manual tests.
- Shopify had ~8400 unit tests, ~2300 screenshot tests and ~20 E2E tests.
- Ford (Ford Pass / Lincoln Way) had ~20,000 unit tests, lots of snapshot tests, no UI tests and lots of manual tests.
- Target has ~10,000 unit tests, thorough beta testing with ~10,000 people and additional manual tests.
- Uber had thousands of unit tests, thousands of snapshot tests, a handful of UI tests and manual tests.
- Lyft had thousands of unit tests, a few snapshot tests, a few UI tests and manual tests.

- Avito (classifieds in Russia) had ~2,000 unit tests, ~1,000 component tests, ~750 E2E tests and manual tests.

Automated testing infrastructure using real devices is another challenge that each company needs to solve in a way that works for it. Larger places might invest in building out their own device lab and this is an approach that has large upfront and ongoing costs.

Cloud-based smartphone farms will be more practical for many teams. Examples of this include Google's Firebase Test Lab, or Microsoft's App Center Test, as well as many smaller and larger vendors.

Automated testing could be an article — or book! — in its own right. Here is more food for thought from a variety of sources:

- Better Android Testing Series from Airbnb
- A Framework For Speedy and Scalable Development Of Android UI Tests from Doordash
- Faster testing on Android with Mobile Test Orchestrator from LinkedIn
- Android UI automation from Slack
- The iOS test pyramid from LinkedIn
- Build effective unit tests from Google
- Robot pattern testing on iOS from Capital One
- The page object pattern from Wantedly Engineering
- Two Years of UI testing by Tomas Camin and Francesco Bigagnoli (Swift Heroes, 2018)
- Testing for success in the real world by Donn Felker (Android Summit 2019)
- Testing strategies discussions at the Mobile Native Foundation

Resources for this chapter:
go.mobileatscale.com/17

18

MANUAL TESTING

When starting with a small app, manual testing each release is a viable path. As the app grows, this effort gets more tedious. At scale, for an app that is released weekly, with many engineers working on it, this approach will break down. The goal at scale is to always have a shippable master with zero, or as close to zero, dependency upon manual testing.

There are a few challenges even when manual testing is done by choice, either because it is not (yet) a large overhead, or because there are not enough automated tests in place to allow this testing.

- **Who does manual testing?** When I started at Uber, the engineering team owned all the manual testing for their features. We kept a simple Google Form in place, with basic instructions, recording "pass" or "fail". We repeated the checklist every week as part of the build train. Of course, as we grew, this approach did not scale well, and we started to rely on a release / test team.
- **How do you keep testing instructions up-to-date?** Regardless of who does the testing — an engineer or a

dedicated person — you want clear and simple instructions. You also need test accounts, their login information, and the data to input in each test step. Where will you store this? Who will keep it up to date? At Uber, the platform team built a manual test administration system with which engineering teams would record test instructions, and testers would mark the test as executed or failed every week.

- **To keep manual testing in-house, outsource, or to mix?** At Uber, I calculated how much it cost us engineers to execute manual tests every week. This number was high enough to justify staffing this effort with dedicated people. During my time there, we used both third parties like Applause, and a dedicated in-house quality team. In-house teams are less effort to start with and can access in-house systems. On the other hand, third parties can be more reliable and scale up or down based on how much testing you need.
- **How do you integrate manual testing in your build train and release process?** How do you handle issues found? What type of issue should block the release, and what are things that will not? You need to incorporate the manual testing step into your release workflow.

A frequent headache with manual tests is how regressions are found at the eleventh hour, right before release. This is still better than the alternative of releasing with new regressions. Still, it can put engineers under pressure to fix a bug quickly, to avoid the release from being delayed. The root cause of the bug can often be hard to locate, as it might be a week or more since the offending code was merged.

If this "last-minute bug report" issue is hitting you or your team frequently, consider reducing the time to get feedback. For example, could manual testing start earlier? Could it run parallel to development? Can it happen continuously for key scenarios? Should engineers execute some basic tests? Can automation help more?

When you have a manual testing process in place, make sure to leave enough time not just for testing, but also for fixing any high-impact bugs. Do this either by doing manual testing early and leaving buffer time for fixing, or by being flexible and pushing back the app release schedule if you find regressions.

Manual tests stay essential for mobile apps in a few cases, even companies which invest in best-in-class automation and spare no time and effort agree.

- **Interfacing with the physical world**. When relying on camera input for recognizing patterns like QR codes, doing document scanning, or AR, you can automate much of the tests but will still need to do manual verification. The same applies for applications utilizing NFC.

- **End-to-end testing of payments systems**. I spent four years at Uber working on payments. Automation of payments tests has a catch-22: payments fraud systems are sophisticated enough to detect and ban suspicious patterns, such as things that look seemingly automated. This means they quickly ban automated tests. You could test against test harnesses for payments providers, but then you are not testing against production. Deciding if you invest in working around payments fraud systems or investing more in monitoring, alerting, and staged rollouts of payments changes will depend on your situation. At Uber, we moved towards the former.

- **Exploratory testing.** Great QA teams and vendors excel at this scenario. They attempt to "break" the app using creative steps that do not occur to engineers, but which end users will employ, regardless. Except that unlike users — who often quietly churn and do not report anything — these testers will provide detailed steps for reproducing all issues. For apps with millions of users, exploratory testing is an area to invest in. The only question is how frequently to do it and how much budget or time to spend on it.t.

There is far more to talk about with testing, and I recommend the book Hands-On Mobile App Testing by Daniel Knott to go deeper into automated and manual testing. This book covers test strategies, tooling, rapid mobile release cycles, testing throughout the app lifecycle, and more.

Resources for this chapter:
go.mobileatscale.com/18

PART III

CHALLENGES DUE TO LARGE ENGINEERING TEAMS

Building an app with a small team is very different than doing so with 10, 20, or more, mobile engineers. Lots of problems that seemed insignificant with a small team, become much larger.

Ensuring consistency in architecture becomes much more challenging. If your company builds multiple apps, how do you balance not rewriting everything from scratch while moving at a fast pace, over waiting on "centralized" teams?

The larger the mobile team, the more builds become a problem. Larger teams usually mean more code and slower build times. With a large team, the cost of a slow build can mean engineering months — or years! — wasted doing nothing. Finding tooling that supports a large mobile engineering team becomes increasingly difficult and some teams will resort to building custom solutions, when they cannot find vendors who support their scale of use cases.

Let's go through the challenges that become more pressing as your mobile engineering team grows in size.

19

PLANNING AND DECISION MAKING

When you work on a small mobile team with a handful of engineers, you just go and build the new features. You probably discuss decisions with each other and comment on code reviews, but that is about it. With a larger team, this process will have to change, both to avoid stepping on each others' toes and to keep the code and architecture choices consistent.

Formalizing the planning process is a practice worth introducing above a certain team size. I have seen companies do this when they have only a few mobile engineers, and other firms delay it until they have up to 30 native engineers. Uber started an RFC planning process early on when there were less than a handful of mobile engineers.

You probably want to formalize the specification phase before, or at the same time, as the engineering planning phase. A large part of project delays come from unclear requirements and scope creep, and being unclear on what the business wants to build. This is usually done by product managers starting up a PRD (Product Requirements Document) process, this document being a formal, "you can now start work" step with engineering. See this list of examples of how various companies approach PRDs.

iOS and Android teams working together on planning is such a big win for efficiency, and yet in many companies, these teams work in silos. By planning features together, you ensure both teams build the same functionality and iOS and Android engineers learn about the differences between platforms. You can standardize things like feature flags, analytic events naming, and, perhaps, even class structure. Engineers can review each others' code, and an iOS engineer might be able to point out an incorrectly implemented business case in the Android code. A win for everyone!

At Uber, one of the major advantages of using RIBs as our architecture was how the structure of the app and components were very similar across iOS and Android. This made shared planning a given and something we just did, without even thinking about it. Why would you not do so?

Decision paralysis is a situation that comes up with teams that start to get good — and thorough — with planning. I have observed teams doing a thorough analysis of the problem space and alternatives, then delaying making a decision.

I suggest timeboxing planning, and in the end, going with the most sensible approach, given the information you gathered. I have noticed diminishing returns in spending more time on planning, instead of building in short iterations and getting feedback on whether your plans work or not. This is especially true on mobile — where you can run into tooling and framework issues — shifting to spend time on prototyping can often be more useful than whiteboarding further approaches.

Getting the "signal to noise ratio" right is a problem many teams and companies worry about planning. Teams are often hesitant to work on a new feature, as they do not want to create too much noise. Executives sometimes worry whether their teams can focus on shipping features, after those teams start to broadcast plans more openly.

I have personally only seen downsides of working in silos. At Microsoft, this was the case back in 2014. At Uber, I was surprised to see the "broadcast to all" model work exceptionally well. Whenever a mobile team was about to build a new feature, they sent an "Intent for RFC" summary to a mobile-only RFC mailing list. Almost all of the 300+ mobile engineers at Uber were on this list. Then, once the RFC was ready to review, they emailed this list as well. This process helped to catch problems early. It also spread knowledge fast and even helped people decide on moving teams to areas which they were more passionate about!

I have since advised startups and mid-sized companies on starting a design doc or RFC process and my advice — in brief — runs like this:

- Define a design document template for a given stack (e.g. for mobile, backend, or web).
- Get most engineers on board with the idea.
- Start writing short docs and sending them out to everyone, as well as making it clear who the required approvers are.
- Over-communicate rather than under-communicate. Prefer lightweight process and tooling to heavyweight ones.
- Observe what happens, and iterate based on the reaction.

If your mobile team is not yet planning with lightweight design docs or RFCs: consider giving this approach a go.

Resources for this chapter:
go.mobileatscale.com/19

20

ARCHITECTING WAYS TO AVOID STEPPING ON EACH OTHER'S TOES

I have not mentioned mobile architecture until now. Is it not an important consideration, even when apps are small? In my experience, while a team is small, architecture really does not matter that much. As long as you choose a structure that is testable enough, you'll be fine with MVP, MVVM, MVC, VIPER, or a similar approach.

Back in the day, the old Uber app followed the "Apple MVC" approach on iOS and MVP on Android. While pain points kept growing with the number of engineers, the app grew to almost 100 native engineers working with this architecture, before bigger architecture changes were made, migrating to RIBs.

The trouble starts when too many engineers end up modifying the same files. In the case of the early Uber app, this file was the presentation / view logic of the on-trip page. This was a screen where up to 50 engineers made changes, and accidentally broke each other's functionality. We tried to break the page down into smaller components, but component communication and navigation conflicts kept arising.

Building an architecture that supports hundreds of mobile engineers collaborating on the same codebase is not trivial. The team at Uber spent half a year prototyping and experimenting with different approaches, from the usual suspects, all the way to (B)-VIPER. In the end, we built our own and open-sourced the architecture known as RIBs. We optimized the architecture to work for a large number of engineers and many nested states. The architecture uses immutable models that re-emit values across the app whenever possible. The architecture was not just diagrams. We built tooling to deal with the increased complexity from code generation tooling to onboarding tutorials.

With a large team, architecture is a means to control the level of isolation between teams and components, limiting overlaps and accidental conflicts while increasing complexity and lines of code. Maybe MVP, MVVP, (B)VIPER, RIBs, or another better-known approach works well enough for your team. If it doesn't, start to formalize which solution would work, why, and what the tradeoffs would be.

You can formalize your approach in various ways:

- **Verbal agreement**: The quickest way. It is also the one that leaves room for most interpretation, and new joiners might not be aware of past discussions.
- **Documenting the approach**: A common method which works well for smaller teams. It is down to each engineer to follow recommendations and for code reviewers to notice when engineers are diverging from this agreement.
- **Tooling to help with formalizing**: You can build frameworks that help with consistency. You could use templates or code generation tools, so that your components are "wired up correctly" at the click of a button. You could also put lint rules in place to automatically catch "architecture violations". The larger the team, the more it can pay off to invest beyond just documenting your approach. At Uber, we built tooling

around component generation and had the lint
certain architecture rules, such as Presenters n(
allowed to know of, or invoke Routers.

Principles you will most likely need to follow in order ᴡ ᴜ₁ ₁
to hundreds of mobile engineers, include:

- Feature isolation
- Monorepo-like code structure. Here is how we did it at
  Uber on iOS and on Android
- Strong code and feature ownership
- Automated tests guarding the app's features

For a mobile architecture to support working at scale — with several
dozen engineers — mistakes need to be clear before merging into
the main branch. Automated tests should catch functionality issues
as part of the pre-merge steps. You need to invest in an architecture
that supports this kind of testability and keeps a high level of test
coverage. Engineers should be confident in merging changes,
knowing they did not break other parts of the app.

Resources for this chapter:
go.mobileatscale.com/20

Look up
an hitectures her
MVP
MVVP

B-VIPER
RIBs

21

SHARED ARCHITECTURE ACROSS SEVERAL APPS

If your company builds several apps, they will all start with different architecture. Different teams will be building each of the apps, moving fast in the early days. However, the idea of having a more "unified" architecture will come up, over time. The sooner there are mobile platform teams owning shared components such as experimentation, feature flags, performance, and others, the sooner this idea is likely to surface.

While a unified architecture will no doubt have clear benefits at this point, it will mean a lot of work such as possibly rewriting a good part of the app. This is a classic paradox: in order to prove the benefits of a shared architecture, we need to be on a shared architecture.

A sensible middle ground is to start making steps towards a unified architecture, but without a rewrite. Here are the benefits in unifying the architecture between the iOS and Android apps:

- **Shared language.** Can we start to "unify" how iOS and Android talks about architecture as a first step? Can we agree on how to name concepts such as screens, navigations, modals, flows?

- **Shared planning**. Can we start to do formal, but lightweight planning with design documents? Can we plan the same feature for iOS and Android in the same document?
- **Breaking down silos**. Are mobile teams in the organization talking to each other, even when working on different apps? If not, how can they start to have conversations? For example, could we start cross-team planning reviews or other collaboration?
- **One shared component at a time.** What is a good candidate in terms of functionality or library that can be shared across apps? If this is built in-house, can it start to use a more "unified" architecture approach between iOS and Android?
- **Introduce new architecture concepts in new parts of the app**. Who said you need to rewrite the app for a new architecture? Can you not start to build new screens with a new approach? This is similar to taking a pragmatic approach to moving languages. For example, when introducing Swift in an Objective C codebase, without rewriting the existing code.

Migrating to a new mobile architecture is expensive. After weighing the cost versus the upside, most teams will decide against going all-in on a new architecture, and they are usually right to do so. The only time I recommend a rewrite is when major changes are to be made for the app, when much of the codebase needs to be touched. Even then, rewrites will usually take longer, and will be more painful than you originally budget for.

The behind-the-scenes story of Uber's rewrite to Swift and the pain points along the way, has had a fair bit of discussion online. This was my first project at Uber, and also the largest rewrite I have been part of. The rewrite made sense, as the UX changes were cross-cutting and impacted almost all workflows and app parts. Still, if it was not for the major design and UX change, I am not convinced Uber would have done the rewrite and architecture change.

While Uber rewrote the Rider app using RIBs in 2016 and later did a full rewrite with the Driver App in 2018, the Eats app still remains on the "existing" architecture. During my time, there wasn't a strong enough business case to justify stopping work and making under-the-hood-changes that don't impact the user experience, and I agreed with this assessment. Following a pragmatic approach, many of the new components were being built with RIBs. A RIBs adapter was also built, so components using RIBs can be shared across multiple Uber apps, regardless of what architecture they are on.

Resources for this chapter:
go.mobileatscale.com/21

22

TOOLING MATURITY FOR LARGE ENGINEERING TEAMS

Companies whose apps are compiled from millions of lines of code usually also set up a mobile platform team. At this scale, the company will have dozens of native engineers working on apps. They will run into the problem of native development tools starting to have performance or process issues at this scale, with no good off-the-shelf solutions. This was the case at Uber, and I hear companies like Facebook, Spotify, and many others face the same issue.

Build time at this scale is one of the biggest problems. By "at scale," I mean building a project with a few million lines, and doing this a dozen times per engineer, times a hundred or more engineers. Throw in running a full automation test suite, and it is not hard to justify hiring a few people to build something that is better than what most services have to offer.

Should you use Bazel, Buck, Gradle, or xcodebuild? What are optimizations you can make on the build? This problem will keep engineers busy, especially as the build tools area is an ever-evolving one.

When you have 50 mobile engineers working on the codebase, cutting the build time by 30 seconds could mean "gaining" several "engineer months" per year. Do the math: assuming engineers build the app five times a day, multiplied by the number of engineers, this comes to two hours "spent idle" every day across the team, or three months every year. The investment of an engineer spending a few weeks to get this reduction makes perfect sense, as does having engineers regularly revisit the build performance.

The workflow of shipping more than a few apps is also challenging. Each app needs to have checkpoints from the build being cut, through test phases such as localization tests, manual and smoke tests, performance tests, beta users, and others. Orchestrating this process for one app is not that difficult. However, keeping track of dozens of build trains across iOS and Android is something that internal tools can do better than anything you can readily buy. You will find yourself needing to make a build or release train for your own needs.

The maturity of tools keeps improving across both iOS and Android and I personally expect more off-the-shelf solutions to become available in the coming years. Still, compare the mobile tooling ecosystem to that on the backend; tooling for large mobile apps seems to be less of a solved problem than for large backend systems.

Resources for this chapter:
go.mobileatscale.com/22

23

SCALING BUILD & MERGE TIMES

Native mobile app build times quickly become problem areas with most projects. iOS engineers are unfortunately familiar with how seemingly slow Xcode builds projects, and Android engineers with a project beyond "Hello, World" will also start to count the seconds and then the minutes, on a build.

Neither Apple nor Google have prioritized build time improvements for large projects. This is especially true for projects with hundreds of thousands, or millions, of lines of code and dozens of dependencies.

Luckily, there are tools to make build times faster, but they take time to integrate, tweak, and fit into the "one-click-build" workflow. Bazel is the tool that is becoming the most popular among companies building mobile at scale. Many companies are in the process of moving to Bazel from Buck or Gradle: Grab, Uber, Pinterest, and the Android AOSP platform are examples of companies and projects moving over. Even with Bazel, there is plenty of work to do to speed up the build. The more mobile engineers there are in a company, the more it can make sense to have them work part-time or full-time on improving the app build experience.

Focusing on build improvements becomes a must, on a per-platform level, as the mobile developer team grows. There are several low-hanging fruits which teams like this can tackle, and other, more complex ones. An example of a lower hanging fruit is how on iOS, dynamic frameworks can be costly both for build times, for app size and for cold launch time. When shorter build times and the smaller app size is a priority, it is worth switching to static libraries. A more expensive way to implement change is moving to a monorepo.

Whether to keep using distributed source code vs moving to a monorepo is a question that teams at the size of between 20 to 40 engineers start to ask. Most teams start with pulling in dependencies and libraries from different repositories, doing this before compile time. The time to download dependencies through the network is time-consuming, so caching is used to optimize this approach.

As the codebase and the number of engineers grows, the time spent fetching dependencies keeps growing. Suddenly, the idea of having all dependencies live in the same monorepo seems less crazy. There are still no great monorepo tools for mobile as of 2021, so you would have to build much of this yourself.

At Uber, we moved to a monorepo for Android and one for iOS, when we hit around 100 native engineers per platform. Should you do the same? Unfortunately, there is no definite answer, only trade-offs to consider. What is more important for your team? Short build times, standardized versioning, or keeping the investment low on custom tooling or mobile platform teams?

Keeping master green - at scale. How difficult is it to keep short the time for merging changes, and to keep the main branch always green? If you have builds that execute fast — say, fifteen minutes to run all tests — and few merges per day — say 10 or 20 — this is no challenge.

What if your build takes thirty minutes to complete with unit, integration, and UI tests? And what if you have 10 pull requests coming in per hour? Is there a way you can keep both the main branch green and also keep the time to merge low, as close as possible to the thirty minutes minimum?

To make this happen, you need to parallelize both the builds. But is it safe to run two PRs parallel when one could impact the other? This problem leads to a complex but equally exciting problem. At Uber, we ended up building a Submit Queue that breaks up builds into parallel parts. It then does probabilistic modeling on the build queue, determining changes likely to pass and prioritizing these. If this sounds like something you would like to learn more about, you can read the details of this approach in this whitepaper.

While there are probably few companies with the amount of mobile PRs happening daily as Uber had, if you are one of them, you will have to invest in bringing down the average time to merge changes and keep the engineering feedback loops low.

Further reading:

- Keeping master green at scale from Uber
- Developing fast & reliable iOS builds from Pinterest
- Blazing through the super app Bazel migration from Grab
- Modernizing our Android build system from Dropbox
- Static vs dynamic frameworks in Swift from Revolut engineer Andres Cecilia Luque

Resources for this chapter:
go.mobileatscale.com/23

24

MOBILE PLATFORM LIBRARIES AND TEAMS

As the number of mobile engineers working on an app, or in the company, grows, the trend of "reinventing the wheel" tends to emerge. TeamA will need a piece of functionality, such as logging, analytics, data storage etc and they will make their own choices and choose their own implementation. Then TeamB faces the same challenge. Assuming they talk with TeamA, they will probably decide it makes sense to reuse what TeamA did, not just for them, but for other teams.

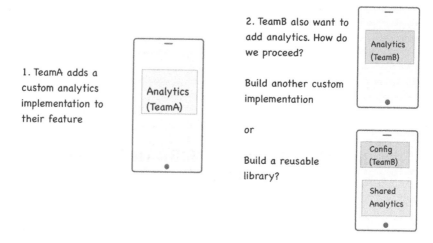

Build a reusable component, or another custom implementation? A common question, as apps grow.

Internal mobile libraries are usually created sooner rather than later, during the development of apps. In many cases, the internal library might just be a lightweight wrapper around a vendor solution, written with the goal of easy migration to another solution, should the need arise.

There is no limit to what can be in an internal library, but common internal libraries can include:

- Logging
- Analytics
- Data persistence
- Feature flags, A/B testing & experimentation
- Networking & authentication
- Testing: UI testing, unit testing, mock generation
- Brand UI elements, colors, themes
- UI elements, frameworks & layouts.
- Message display
- Animations
- Image management
- Navigation frameworks

- Architecture frameworks
- Performance monitoring / profiling tools
- Push notifications
- Shared functionality specific to app domains: calling, PDFs, scanning, location, maps, and others

Maintaining these libraries usually becomes difficult as the team — and the number of libraries built internally — grows. As engineers, we often think that the main challenge is to build the library itself and migrate existing use cases over to it. However, most teams find out just how painful maintenance can be, but only years after the library has been written.

The main problems with maintenance are usually these:

1. **The original engineers are no longer with the team**. This could become a problem in a few ways. The knowledge might be missing on how to modify the code. Still, other engineers can usually understand code that was written to be used by others, so this is rarely the problem. The bigger issue is that when the original engineers have left, changes often come in unchecked. This results in the next issue.

2. **The quality of the library diminishes following a series of short-term fixes.** When a team comes across an issue that they can fix by a change to the shared library, they often go for a short-term fix. As long as there is an owner of the library, this owner can decide not to allow low-quality or short-term fixes.

3. **The owning team has no bandwidth for maintenance or migrations.** Another common problem is a product team building several of these components. However, their plate is full of product work, and engineers can barely get time for small maintenance work. If major changes would need to be done, there is no one to take this on.

Creating mobile platform teams when the number of mobile engineers is large enough is a common solution to the ownership and maintenance problem. There is no "golden rule" on the size at which this should happen but most companies make this step when they have — or expect to have — between 20 and 30 mobile engineers.

Mobile platform team ownership can vary greatly, based on what is considered "common" in the company. Areas common to be owned by a dedicated mobile platform are the ones listed below. Note that platform teams usually own several of these.

- **Mobile build infrastructure**, especially when deciding to keep the builds in-house. Even when using a third-party vendor, a mobile infra team might own the vendor relationship, and the setup of the builds.
- **App Store release management**. At companies with mature release processes, this area often includes owning the manual testing process after the build cut, dogfooding/beta processes, and the process for last-minute hotfixes.
- **Developer tooling & experience**. At scale, with 15 or more engineers working on apps with hundreds of thousands of lines, the limitations of the "default" tooling start to become more painful. Building the app or running tests becomes slower, both locally and on the CI. Speeding up these steps is no longer just a "quick change", but one that could need more complex tooling changes, code structure changes, or both.
- **Architecture & architecture maintenance**. The first non-infra platform team tends to take ownership of the app's architecture, ensuring it is built in a maintainable way. This team often becomes both a guide to help less experienced engineers make sustainable design decisions, and also a "policing force" which ensures the architecture stays clean, and in line with the broader vision. Dependency management, code quality governance,

testability — and testing — will often fall under this umbrella.

- **SDKs** used within or outside the company. SDKs are usually specific to the business and to the needs of the teams.
- **Mobile app reliability & performance**, from crash rates, networking reliability, logging and performance monitoring.
- **Building capabilities to enable developers** to be more efficient. With mobile frameworks — and even languages — evolving quickly, much of the ecosystem has gaps. The larger the team, the more visible these gaps are. Several mobile platform teams decide it is worth building a solution, when the tooling they could buy is not good enough. Examples of this can include building a custom UI testing framework, putting a device lab in place, or implementing a build train that integrates with bespoke tools across the company.
- **Shared internal library ownership.** Once mobile platform teams are in place, they tend to take over — or build — some of the internal mobile libraries.

Here are a few guidelines on running a healthy mobile platform team:

- **Clear mission.** Ensure the platform team has a well-defined mission that is more specific than "own all the shared stuff". Examples of missions could be "Enable mobile engineers to work more efficiently, month after month" or "Ship the most reliable app in our industry."
- **Clear goals.** The platform team should have measurable goals on the areas they want to include. Possible goals include range reliability targets, percentage of teams using shared components, lines of code to integrate certain features, number of projects open-sourced, and others. A platform team without goals will

struggle to decide where to focus, and will become less efficient than one that knows where it is going, and how it will get there.

- **Sufficient staffing.** The team should be big enough so that they have bandwidth to do "product" work on the platform, on top of providing support for the rest of the organisation.
- **Clear contracts** between platform and non-platform teams. The platform team should be clear on what they do, and what they do not own, and this should be a shared — and agreed upon — understanding.
- **Clear support channels.** Engineers should know where and how they can get support from the platform team. This could be shared chat groups, office hours, dedicated people to ping and most likely, a combination for all of these.
- **Clear process for engagement.** The platform team should make it clear how product teams can work with them for feature requests; how to make the request, who and how will prioritize this work, and how they can track the status.

As inspiration, here are examples of how companies approached mobile platform teams. Note that some of the examples are anecdotal, and others might have changed how they operate. Do not forget that each company solves its own problems, taking its people and other constraints into account. Do not blindly copy what other companies are doing, follow the setup that will result in the right level of leverage you need.

- **Uber** had a platform team owning mobile developer experience, including development tooling and build systems. Another team called Mobile Platform owned the architecture and shared services (RIBs and internal additions like experimentation framework). Mobile Platform later split to App Platform (owning app metric / reliability / performance, architecture and Core modules governance) and Mobile Foundations (owning reusable components and frameworks).

- **UberEats** was a "startup" within Uber, operating almost fully independently from the rest of Uber in the early years. UberEats was started in 2015, and the first "official" mobile platform team was created four years later, in 2019. Even before this first platform team, UberEats teams all "pitched in" to build components that other teams would use in a reusable fashion.
- **Twitter** used to have an iOS and Android foundation team with a few workstreams each. As the size increased, these teams split into smaller teams within each foundation, like UI, performance, architecture, builds, and developer experience.
- **Amazon** has a platform team owning app architecture, logging, metrics, and shared, "infrastructure-like" features. Major features are often spun off for experience teams to own. These experience teams have contracts with the platform to bring clarity on code ownership and how design and code reviews are done.
- **Just Eat** has an iOS and an Android platform team. These teams own all of the "typical" platform work, as well as the release process for iOS or Android.
- **Skyscanner** has a Mobile Infra team (owning CI/CD, build and release management) and a Mobile Core team (owning reusable libraries and helping with issues impacting multiple teams).
- **VMware** has a small team building mobile UI components and another team owning SDKs used internally, and by third parties.
- **Zenly** (a Snap company) has a mobile platform team consisting of both mobile and backend engineers. They found that the nature of much of the mobile platform work spans from the app level, to the backend. Examples of this include changing the networking layer for a different transport mechanism than TCP, metrics across the app and

backend, custom crash reporting, remote debugging, and other advanced functionality.

- **Walmart** has an iOS and an Android mobile platform team, which owns all platform-specific work. This meant from mobile CI/CD pipelines, through testing, debug and performance tooling, crash reporting, security practices, and dependency management, all the way to UI navigation elements or analytics. The platform team maintains a long list of capabilities they own.
- **N26** has a "Core" iOS and a "Core" Android one, these teams owning all shared capabilities. They later explored splitting this team into smaller cross-functional teams, starting with a Design System team.
- **Sixt** has a platform team for iOS, Android and web. This team takes care of all the common tasks like mono-repos, CI/CD, observability, architecture, libraries, etc. They choose to combine mobile and web because there are many similar parts, such as CI/CD or libraries. This helped with knowledge sharing and reducing duplications.
- **Booking.com** has several teams working together on what they call the "App Core Platform." One team owns core components and services, and a different one owns the build and release processes, including testing and app stability. A third team looks purely at app performance such as startup time and time-to-interactive, for important screens, while the fourth team looks after the in-house development frameworks used by product-focused teams. All teams have a mix of iOS and Android engineers. Finally, this organization also has a team of backend developers who look after the app's backends from an overall governance perspective, making sure all the backends called by the Booking.com apps are healthy and reliable.

When to spin off the first mobile platform team is always a challenge. Large mobile teams clearly need one or more of these teams. But what about teams that are still small? Would you want to spin a platform team off when you have 15 engineers?

Starting a platform team too late can mean lots of redundancy in the code, poor abstractions and little reusability between identical functionality. Were a platform team in place earlier, this team would have been the natural owner of several shared features, and would have also taken ownership of the app-wide architecture.

Starting a platform team too early has the drawback of making it hard to make a business case for it. Why hire an engineer who will *not* ship product work? Additionally, the first platform team usually draws the most experienced engineers. These engineers are often also the most productive *product* engineers. Even if the company hires new engineers, these original engineers often leave a gap for a few months on the product teams.

I write more advice on starting and running a mobile platform team as an engineering manager, in the book Growing as a Mobile Engineer.

PART IV

LANGUAGES AND CROSS-PLATFORM APPROACHES

The tooling to build mobile apps keeps changing. New languages, frameworks, and approaches that all promise to address the pain points of mobile engineering keep appearing.

But which approach should you choose? Should you use Objective C or Swift to build iOS apps? Java or Kotlin for Android? Or should you invest in a cross-platform approach that promises a "write once, run everywhere" approach like Flutter, React Native, Cordova? Or perhaps settle for a middle ground, or reuse business logic written in Kotlin, C#, C++ or other languages?

In this section, we cover the most common industry choices regarding languages, frameworks, and cross-platform approaches when building mobile apps. There is no shortage of tools on how to build apps. It will be down to the constraints and tradeoffs you are willing to make in the approach you choose, for building across iOS, Android - and possibly other - platforms.

25

ADOPTING NEW LANGUAGES AND FRAMEWORKS

When should we onboard to a new language? Should we start to use a new and promising framework? Unfortunately, there are no simple answers and even when you do your research, you might regret the decision you take.

The more complex your app, the more risky adopting a new language is, or switching over to a different "core" framework can be. By "core" framework, I mean a framework that is used across the apps, such as networking libraries, dependency injection frameworks, libraries implementing business logic cross-platform, and others.

In 2016, Swift was at version 2.2. The engineering team at Uber decided to go 100% with Swift when rewriting Uber's Rider app. The decision was almost a disaster, mainly because the team did not expect the binary size for Swift to be multiple times that of Objective C. Former mobile platform manager Chris Brauchli explains the problems in more detail in this post.

Having learned from the experience, Uber took far more care to evaluate every aspect of adopting a new language. For Kotlin, the team did extensive evaluations and performance measurements.

GERGELY OROSZ

You will want to invest effort to evaluate a new language or framework that is in line with what the work adoption would mean, and the risk it carries. Uber invested a large effort to evaluate Kotlin because rolling it out would have impacted hundreds of Android engineers, and apps that generate billions of dollars of monthly revenue.

Areas which you want to evaluate are similar to how you would evaluate cross-platform frameworks. On top of those considerations, areas worth taking into account are:

- **The maturity of the language / framework**. How stable is the API? Are there success stories of using the language or framework in the wild, which relate to what you are trying to build?
- **Migrations** coming up in the future. If you adopt this language or framework, would you need to migrate existing code over? How large would this effort be?
- **Engineering enthusiasm.** Is this a technology that engineers would be excited to work with? Is there enough support in the team to go ahead with potentially adopting this technology? What proportion of the team is sceptical of the technology, and why?
- **Risks.** What could go wrong? How could this impact the app, customers or the business?

Building a smaller "pilot" project with the new language or framework is a great way to get a better feel for it, and to answer questions about usability, obvious issues and tooling.

My personal approach is supportive of trying out anything new, but in a way that limits the "blast radius". Can we use the new technology in a less important part of the app? Can we experiment in an app that has smaller usage numbers? Could we start by making a change, so that only company employees test this new setup, before we move further?

Mobile engineering keeps evolving, and so will the languages, frameworks and tools that we use. We should be unafraid to try out new approaches and stories like Uber's Swift rewrite should serve as reminders of what can happen when you have no "plan B".

Resources for this chapter:
go.mobileatscale.com/25

26

KOTLIN MULTIPLATFORM AND KMM

Kotlin Multiplatform is one of several approaches to build cross-platform features, or apps, by sharing common code with the Kotlin language. We discuss this approach separately from other cross-platform feature development and app development approaches, thanks to its rapid rise in adoption among large apps and developer teams.

Kotlin Multiplatform was announced in 2017. With it, you can write Kotlin and build:

- JVM libraries for Android, or backend services
- Native framework for iOS and desktop
- JavaScript artifacts for frontend web or backend services

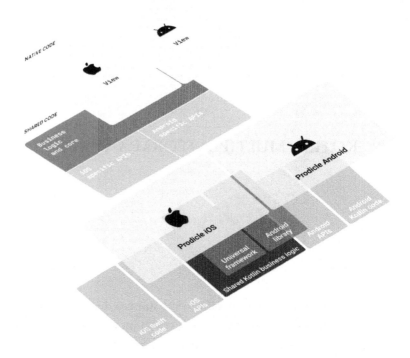

The idea behind Kotlin Multiplatform: share business logic code, keep view code as native. Top: the generic idea. Bottom: how Netflix implemented KMM in their Prodicle TV production app.

Kotlin Multiplatform Mobile (KMM) was released in 2020, and is a tooling layer on top of Kotlin Multiplatform. KMM gives engineers tools for easier IOS and Android development. These tools include:

- Rich IDE integration
- Better debugging capabilities for mobile apps
- Good support for Cocoapods

Touchlab are the global experts in Kotlin Multiplatform Mobile (KMM). Touchlab accelerates KMM adoption through product &

SDK development, early adopter support, architectural & production-readiness reviews and open-source projects.

Touchlab advises enterprises like Square and NBC on scaling KMM and partners with JetBrains to increase KMM adoption. Looking to get started with KMM? Check out their Kotlin Multiplatform starter kit at Touchlab.co.

––––––

Several larger companies have shipped Kotlin Multiplatform projects in production: Netflix, Square, Careem and VMWare being a few of them. There are several benefits of going with this approach:

- **Using Kotlin is a natural choice for many mobile engineers**. Android engineers likely already use it, and it is easy to learn if you already know Swift. It is also beneficial for an iOS engineer to broaden their skills to include Android.
- **KMM encourages fully native UI components.** Unlike the approaches taken by tools such as Flutter and React Native, KMM is designed to allow native mobile developers to build UIs in ways that users and developers are used to.
- **Investment from JetBrains and Google** in the Kotlin Foundation owning the project. This also means first-class support for Kotlin and KMM in JetBrains IDEs and Android Studio.

The case study from Square, which moved Cash App over to Kotlin Multiplatform, highlights reasons why several teams might go with this approach. The Cash App team wanted to keep most of their code as native, and choosing Kotlin as the language for shared components made sense. They started off by collaborating with Touchlab (a sponsor of this book) in testing the technology. They noted how because the platform-agonistic Kotlin resembles Swift, the shift was manageable for iOS engineers. What is more, they had contributions from the server team as well.

Downsides of adopting KMM all come from the technology being less mature. KMM tools are experimental as of 2021, subject to breaking changes that can impact early adopters. Larger teams will find painful tooling gaps. The VMWare team noted that the lack of supported libraries also presented a challenge they eventually overcame.

Among all the cross-platform *feature* development approaches, I see Kotlin Multiplatform and KMM as the most promising. This is the only cross-platform approach where existing native Android engineers feel right at home, and iOS engineers will also have the least steep learning curve in adopting Kotlin and the tooling.

───────

Top-Of-Mind Concerns About KMM

Touchlab Partner Kevin Galligan shares his thoughts on top-of-mind concerns teams have about KMM.

1. Stability. *Will there be breaking changes forcing rework? Will it go away or continue to be improved and maintained?*

Developer experience is critical for adoption of a shared code solution at scale. JetBrains has a track record making some of the world's most popular developer tools in a wide range of ecosystems. We share JetBrains' commitment to the technology: *"After the release of Kotlin 1.4, KMM is in Alpha status. This means the Kotlin team is fully committed to working to improve and evolve this technology and will not suddenly drop it."*

As we continue to help our clients put KMM into production, we'll be keeping close watch on KMM's path to Beta.

2. Dependency Management. *What about modularization, creating and consuming libraries in various configurations?*

Kotlin is native to Android and the preferred language for Android development. Modularization on the Android side follows similar patterns and uses the same tools as 'standard' Android. The Android tooling team is aware of KMP and works along with Jetbrains to ensure compatibility.

On the iOS side, Kotlin is consumed as an Xcode framework and multiple Kotlin modules can be wrapped into one framework. Presently, different Xcode frameworks need to be constructed for different combinations of Kotlin modules. If you have multiple app instances with different combinations of Kotlin modules, you should build and deploy a wrapper Xcode framework for each, rather than publishing an Xcode framework from each Kotlin module. The ability to include multiple Xcode frameworks directly rather than constructing a wrapper framework will continue to be an ongoing discussion with more options in the future.

On the consuming side, teams need to decide if they want to build Kotlin locally or distribute precompiled binaries, which avoids installing and configuring Kotlin tooling and the build time overhead involved. Multiple configuration options are available.

3. iOS DX. *How will the iOS Developer Experience (DX) be impacted?*

KMM is designed to interop directly with platform-native technologies, rather than replacing them, which is why engineers we work with at clients like Square and NBC choose it. Kotlin is exported as an Xcode framework, and Swift/Objc code calls directly into it rather than needing to communicate over some kind of inter-process layer.

We collaborate with JetBrains and others to deliver direct Xcode integration for Kotlin browsing and debugging. The goal is to provide 'native code sharing' vs 'cross platform'. Currently, interop is through an Objective-C interface, although direct Swift interop is planned for future releases.

iOS resources:

- CrashKiOS: crash reporting for Kotlin/Native iOS applications
- Kotlin Native Xcode Plugin: facilitating debugging iOS applications using Kotlin Native in Xcode

To learn how Touchlab can help scale KMM at your organization, please contact them at Touchlab.co.

———

Further reading:

- Kotlin Multiplatform Mobile overview and case studies from Kotlin Multiplatform
- Moving Cash App to Kotlin Multiplatform from Square
- Netflix Android and iOS Studio apps powered by Kotlin Multiplatform from Netflix
- Moving from shared Javascript business logic to Kotlin Multiplatform from Quizlet
- Your multiplatform kaptain has arrived from Careem
- The move to Kotlin Multiplatform from VMWare
- Moving from React Native to Kotlin Multiplatform from Wantendly

Resources for this chapter:
go.mobileatscale.com/26

27

CROSS-PLATFORM FEATURE DEVELOPMENT

Writing the *common* parts of a mobile app once, and reusing it across iOS and Android, is an obvious optimization that comes with several benefits.

- **Reduce the time to build features** by implementing the business logic once. Most people overestimate the time saved in this area. When building for the first time, you still need to test on both platforms. When done right, you save some time, but this is not the biggest of wins.
- **Reduce iOS and Android inconsistencies.** When working separately, iOS and Android teams often implement the business logic in different ways or inconsistently. With shared business logic, this will not happen.
- **Reduced time to maintain** the shared logic. One codebase instead of two.
- **Break down the iOS / Android silos**. In many organizations, iOS and Android teams work in full isolation. Even a little cross-feature development breaks

these silos. I have only seen things go better when iOS and Android engineers talk *more*, not less.

How can you achieve this goal? There are several approaches that allow the writing of business logic once, wrapping it in a library or component, then reusing this logic across both native apps:

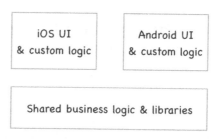

The idea behind cross-platform features and business logic: write the platform-independent logic once, reuse it across apps

There is an ever-growing pool of cross-platform feature development approaches.

Cross-platform architecture using RIBs is the approach we used at Uber. It is an approach in which the iOS and Android codebases are still separate; however, the architecture terminology and tooling are shared. The RIBs' architecture, tooling and training materials are open source and are used by hundreds of companies.

I have built apps using RIBs since before it was released and here are my observations on teams using this approach.

- **Enables cross-platform planning**. One of the biggest benefits of using a shared architecture approach is how you can now design features for both platforms using RFCs or similar approaches. The bulk of how a feature works will be shared and the iOS and Android implementation differences should be called out at this stage.
- **Encourages cross-platform code reviews**. The business logic is still implemented in Swift for iOS and

Java/Kotlin for Android. Still, as engineers are building similar constructs, they can better review each others' code.

- **Encourages onboarding to the "other" platform.** RIBs makes it easier to "pick up" Android if you have been doing iOS. At Uber, I would estimate close to half of the native engineers have contributed on the "other" platform. The cross-platform planning process and code reviews lowered the bar to entry.

- **Tooling is at the heart of this kind of approach.** RIBs ships with component generation for both iOS and Android, taking away manual wiring up of classes. At Uber, we also invested heavily in linting rules that "policed" architectural consistency.

- **The biggest downside** is the "heavyweight" nature of this approach. RIBs brings structure to both the iOS and Android codebases - and this structure can feel limiting to many engineers.

Shared C++ libraries are a battle-tested way to share code — or specialized business logic — across iOS and Android applications. Teams building games, audio and video processing applications and other performance-intensive use cases, are ones which often choose this approach.

At Skype, most of the calling logic was built in C++ from the early days, and shared across all platforms, including for Mac and Windows. Slack followed a similar approach in 2017 with their client apps development, writing, also optimizing and reusing the data fetching, parsing and caching flow logic across iOS, Android, Windows and Linux. PSPDFKit chose C++ as their cross-platform language in 2016 after evaluating other alternatives.

When using C++ components, you need to generate custom headers for both Android (Java) and iOS (Objective C). Djinni is one of the more popular libraries for this and you will have to set up a build pipeline to do this on a continuous basis.

The biggest upsides for choosing C++ is how you can use the library, not just on iOS and Android, but also on Windows, Mac and Linux clients. Having more control over library performance and resource usage is another major upside.

The biggest downside is the barrier to entry. Most native mobile engineers will not be fluent in C++, and you might have engineers on the team who prefer using languages that are less low-level. Putting the right tooling in place could take more effort and you need people with deep C++ expertise to debug and resolve issues as they come up.

Other cross-platform library options include Go Mobile (generating bindings from a Go package and invoking them on Android or iOS), J2ObjC (share business logic written in Java) or using JavaScript and the iOS and Android interpreters, to execute shared JS business logic. All approaches are feasible, although neither have gained much popularity within teams building complex mobile applications.

The lack of visible success stories does not mean you should rule them out: Freshworks chose Go Mobile as their cross-platform approach and were generally happy with the outcome. Their biggest pain point was not the technology, but some native mobile engineers being unhappy with having to maintain a Go codebase.

The more complex your app, the more reasons you will find to consider cross-platform business logic. RIBs can be a good first step toward breaking down iOS and Android silos, but without moving to a new technology. Kotlin Multiplatform is a very promising technology for teams which want to embrace the modern Kotlin language. And C++ is a battle-tested language that is especially useful for apps where the business logic is not only shared on mobile, but on desktop as well.

Do not underestimate the overhead of sharing cross-platform code. Until 2019, Dropbox shared code between iOS and Android using C++. However, they found that the overhead of writing code in a non-standard fashion, ended up being more expensive than just writing the code twice. They shared their challenges on their engineering blog. The overhead of custom frameworks and libraries, a custom development environment, platform differences, and the overhead of training, hiring and retraining developers were all reasons that made Dropbox align its practices with industry standards.

Many companies adopting cross-platform code sharing tend to especially underestimate the cost of losing great, native mobile engineers. For example, if your language of choice for shared components is not Swift or Kotlin, you are likely to lose some of the strongest native iOS or Android engineers on your team; the people who want to work in cutting-edge, native environments.

Further reading:

- RIBs: Uber's cross-platform mobile architecture from Uber
- Architecting Uber's new Driver app using RIBs from Uber
- LibStack: the C++ library foundation for client application architecture from Slack
- Djinni connect C++ with Java or Objective-C declarations from Dropbox
- C++: a pragmatic approach to cross-platform from PSPPDKKit
- The (not so) hidden cost of sharing code between iOS and Android from Dropbox
- Our journey towards cross-platform development with Go Mobile from Freshworks

Resources for this chapter:
go.mobileatscale.com/27

28

CROSS-PLATFORM APP DEVELOPMENT VERSUS NATIVE

Writing business logic and libraries in a shared language allows keeping mobile UIs native, while sharing the code for the business logic. Cross-platform app development frameworks like Flutter, React Native or Cordova leave you no choice but to share the UI layer of the app. For apps that want to be more sophisticated, or have more control at the native UI level, cross-platform business logic solutions might make more sense.

Motivations to consider for a cross-platform app development approach:

- **The "need for speed"**. The frustration with how long it can take to build a feature on both platforms. Would it not be great to work with an approach that promises faster feature development time, and does it on both platforms?
- **The desire to have one engineer ship to two platforms**, instead of needing two engineers. To ship the simplest of UI changes, two engineers need to make two separate changes on two platforms. Both need to be tested, and the rollouts often need to be coordinated. Would it not be nice if the same person could do both?

- **The desire for iOS and Android apps to work exactly the same**. The iOS and Android app for the same product will often differ in small ways. A bug will be present in Android, but not on iOS. Would it not be great for both apps to work in an identical way?
- **Unifying the look and feel of the iOS and Android apps**. Over time, the design team will advocate for a shared UI/UX approach. This will make a lot of sense from both a brand point of view, as well as reducing the design work of two platforms to a unified platform.
- **The desire for "hot reload"**, over waiting on build trains. Even the smallest mobile app change takes weeks to ship due to the code changes needing to be shipped through the App Store. Would it not be wonderful to have the option of experimenting or shipping bug fixes without having to wait on the build train?

While cross-platform feature development helps with unifying much of the business logic between iOS and Android apps, cross-platform app development goes a step further, by unifying the UI layer between the two platforms. There are several technologies with which you could choose to build your app cross-platform. Here are the most popular ones.

Flutter is the framework that seems to have the most momentum for adoption so far in 2021. BMW has fully transitioned to Flutter, and eBay Motors and Nubank have chosen Flutter as their cross-platform app development technology. Google is investing heavily in Flutter and is building most of its new apps only using this technology, at a scale of dogfooding that no other cross-platform app development approach has.

The biggest downside is how you have to learn and develop with Dart to use it. The language is easy enough to pick up and outside of this, there seem to be few reasons to not invest in this approach. Flutter is the most mature cross-platform *app* development approach on the market as of 2021, and the fact that several companies are going all-in for Flutter for app development is a testament for this approach.

Examples of companies using Flutter:

- Google building Google Pay, Stadia, Google Ads, and Google Nest Hub
- eBay Motors app case study: moving to Flutter and writing 220,000 lines of Dart code
- Nubank migration to Flutter: their approach, progress, and the rapid launch their LifeInsurance app
- BMW moving over to one single Flutter codebase, as told by Jorge Coca at Droidcon
- A showcase of Flutter apps collected by Google

React Native had strong momentum in 2016, but in 2018, Airbnb moved off it after investing two years to make it work. In a detailed postmortem, they shared the technical and organizational issues they faced. Shopify, however, announced taking a bet on React Native in 2020, but with a much more cautious approach than several other companies took.

Other big tech companies like Microsoft with Office and Skype, Coinbase, Tesla and Amazon are taking the same cautious approach to introducing React Native in parts of their apps. Amazon even has its own internal React Native conference, with hundreds of engineers using React Native on some projects.

React Native is a good approach for companies with lots of existing web engineers and people familiar with using JavaScript to build native mobile apps. Many of the apps built with RN start as MVPs, or standalone and less complex apps. As the technology matures, we can expect to see more complex apps built and maintained with this approach.

Examples of companies using React Native, or moving off it:

- Shopify and their cautious investment in React Native.

Shopify will not rewrite existing apps, will keep hiring native engineers, and seem to be doing one-off React Native experiments, such as how they launched the Shopify Compass app using React Native, and are also building the Shopify Ping Android version using React Native.
- Wix building their app fully on React Native.
- UberEats building the Restaurant Dashboard app. Note that this is the only Uber app as of 2021 that uses React Native.
- Airbnb moving off React Native: Three years of learning. The story of how Airbnb adopted React Native, and why they moved off of it.

Xamarin/MAUI is a popular cross-platform framework using C#. Microsoft announced "refreshing" Xamarin as the .NET MAUI framework in late 2021. Companies with C# codebases have seen great success in sharing code across backend and native apps with this framework.

Xamarin is a viable alternative for .NET shops and companies with C# engineers, to bootstrap apps. The community around Xamarin is much smaller than Flutter or React Native. However, thanks to Microsoft investing in the platform, it is likely this approach will keep growing in popularity.

Examples of companies using Xamarin/MAUI:

- DraftKings building their Sportsbook and Casino apps
- BBVA — one of the biggest banks in Spain — building its Valora View app
- Philips building its VitaHealth Engage platform

Other cross-platform frameworks include Cordova (formerly PhoneGap), Ionic and NativeScript. There are fewer public case studies for complex apps to be built on these technologies. One of the larger applications built on Cordova/Ionic is the Rabobank application used by roughly half a million customers in the Netherlands. The biggest obstacles to the adoption of these technologies for large-scale projects are usually performance and tooling concerns.

The promises of cross-platform app development are hard to ignore:

- **Cost**. The biggest benefit. Code once, deploy on iOS, Android, and, ideally, on the web and desktop.
- **Reusability**. Reuse code between the two platforms, and perhaps also the web.
- **Novelty** and a cool, new technology to try out. We engineers often get excited by working with something new and interesting like an up-and-coming framework.
- **The same functionality** across iOS and Android. No more need to worry about the two apps working differently.
- **Assuming it is easier to hire** or (re-)train web engineers. Several engineering leaders assume that by going with a cross-platform framework, their existing engineers can pick up mobile development quickly, and that fewer people can ship mobile apps on Android and iOS. This is a promise that often does not live up to reality.

There are obvious downsides to this approach - that are visible even at smaller apps:

- **One more thing that can go wrong.** Both React Native and Flutter add another layer on top of the iOS and Android native code. They do abstract some of the complexity: but when you see a bug happening only on one platform, you'll have to debug if the issue is with your code, with React Native/Flutter, or at the platform level.
- **Native code (still) needed** - especially for the advanced parts. Going with a cross-platform framework will not eliminate the need to write native code for semi-advanced cases, or for platform-specific features.
- **Always a step behind.** Every time iOS or Android

introduces a new API, it will take months - if not more - for these frameworks to come up with an abstraction to wrap these APIs. If you're an early adopter of these APIs, you'll have to implement them natively.

There are downsides that you will only see later.

- **Assuming the same engineers** who kicked off the transition **will be around** years later. Several companies have been burnt by making the decision to move to a framework, following the lead of one or two vocal engineers. However, once those engineers left, the team found themselves unsure if they should keep going, or turn back.
- **Most mobile engineers will always favour native**. You will either have a hard time hiring engineers who deeply care about mobile experiences, or they will be grumbling about the cross-platform approach and seeking to move things back to native.
- **The pain of tooling changes** is something that most teams greatly underestimate.
- **Cross-platform frameworks will always limit you more** than going native does, and these limitations will keep coming up. It could be UX, performance or how to get something done; you have to devote a non-trivial amount of time to them.

The tradeoffs are numerous which you need to carefully evaluate before introducing React Native, Flutter, Cordova or other cross-app frameworks with large apps or teams. Here are a few areas you want to evaluate before deciding to introduce these frameworks, or to pass on them.

1. **Performance** versus native. How is app startup time impacted? How quickly do screens load? How much leeway do you have to optimize UI performance?

2. **Development experience** versus native. Is hot reloading supported during development? How quick are changes to test in the developer environment? How good and reliable are developer tools?

3. **Tooling**. How well is debugging supported? Performance and memory profiling? How easy or difficult is it to write automated tests, do linting/static analysis? How is the CI/CD tooling?

4. **Device support** - especially low-end devices. How does the framework perform on older models? How much business does the company or app expect to do on these models?

5. **UX/UX "native" look and feel**, and the tradeoffs around them. Many cross-platform frameworks bring a more "generic" UX that can feel "alien" to how native iOS or Android apps feel. How does the framework do at this level?

6. **Release speed and quality.** How easy is it to ship a release? How quickly can a release be executed? Which quality checks can be automated, and checks does the framework not support?

7. **Binary size** implications. What footprint would using these frameworks add to the app? How much larger would implementing a screen or a class be?

8. **Platform limitations**. What are known issues with iOS and Android platforms and when and how will issues that are important for the app be addressed?

9. **Mixing with native code.** How easy or difficult is it to add in native code? What about the tooling, such as adding in tests and static analysis?

10. **Type safety** for interfaces between the framework and native code. How safely can you pass objects back and forth?

11. **Build performance.** How much slower or faster are builds and running tests? Build speed becomes a sticking point with large developer teams.

12. **Versioning options** in case of hot reload-like solutions with React Native. How can you handle rolling out code only to apps above a certain version?
13. **Autonomy of the mobile team** in making the decision to move forward with the framework. If the decision to use or not a cross-platform framework does not come from the engineering team, you end up with less empowered engineers than when they do make the call.

Several large companies that do not adopt one of the better-known cross-platform frameworks will sometimes implement solutions to solve one or more of the above problems. Or it might be a framework that allows some level of "hot reloading". It might be a cross-platform declarative UI framework. When you have the resources to build something like this, it might be an investment that makes sense. However, when you do not you still need to figure out how pressing these problems are and how you intend to solve them.

The biggest blocker for cross-platform apps at scale seems to be the tooling support, and having to give up UI-level control when going with a cross-platform app solution. Many of the large apps want to keep granular control at the UI level, in order to ensure best-in-class performance, and so to stick with two native codebases, or move towards cross-platform feature development.

Evaluate what *you* need to do instead of copying what other companies are already doing. Both the cross-platform feature development, as well as the app development toolset is evolving at a rapid pace, and you have plenty of approaches to choose from.

To figure out which approach works for you, answer these questions: which are the biggest mobile engineering pain points and what are your constraints? Do cross-platform frameworks tools that come with tradeoffs offer the right type of benefits and acceptable drawbacks for your use case?

Resources for this chapter:
go.mobileatscale.com/28

29

WEB, PWA & BACKEND-DRIVEN MOBILE APPS

Being unable to update mobile apps on the fly is the source of many major pain points for native apps and are ones that we covered in the Mistakes are Hard to Revert and The Long Tail of Old App Versions chapters. But what if we had a magic wand to make this all go away, updating the app in an instant?

Turns out, we do have the magic wand to instantly update mobile apps. A few magic wands, actually.

PWA (progressive web apps) use web browser APIs to build a native-like user experience. PWAs can support having an app shell, push notifications on Android or asset caching. PWAs can be a natural next step to enhance the mobile web. Pinterest is one of the companies which invested early on in building a progressive PWA in an effort to improve their mobile web usage.

For complex apps, PWAs are unlikely to be a replacement for, or competition to native apps. However, it is worth keeping an eye on how the technology evolves.

Embedding web screens into the mobile app is the most common and easiest approach. For parts of the app that you want to have dynamic content, adding a WKWebView on iOS or a WebView on Android can be a sensible way to go. As a note, Apple makes it clear they reject apps that only wrap a website, without adding functionality, but web views within the app with additional business logic is fine.

Building support for when the app is offline is one of the challenges. You have to load the webview content from local data in this case, then sync that local data back when connectivity returns.

The user experience not feeling "natural" to the OS is usually the biggest drawback of this approach. You have to put a lot of effort into styling components so they feel native to your app. Still, with a webview-based approach, you have animations that you cannot replicate, such as the animation when going from the master to the detail view on iOS.

For Android, there are several gotchas to be aware of with this approach, especially on older devices and OS versions. On iOS, using JavascriptCore almost always has performance drawbacks. Lucidchart migrated their hybrid app to WKWebView and saw a 10-15x major performance improvement. Note that for apps that do simple JavaScript operations that take little time, this performance improvement might be less noticeable.

Optimizing the web pages is something you want to invest heavily in order to have good performance for embedded web screens. The UberEats team spent considerable time trimming the content served to what mobile needed, optimizing server-side processing times and measuring the improvements. This effort built upon the many mobile web optimizations the m.uber.com team had done in reducing bundle sizes and dependencies.

Backend-driven mobile apps are a natural next step in making native apps easier to update on-the-fly, but without having to rely on web views or third-party frameworks. When building native apps, you have the best control of the user experience, resource usage and performance. The biggest tradeoff is how you need to ship binary changes in order for the application's business logic to change.

What if the business logic was driven by the backend, while part of the mobile app acts like an application shell that interprets these instructions?

This idea comes around sooner or later for all complex apps. It will spark discussion, especially for areas where the business needs frequent changes, or parts of the app that need to behave slightly differently based on regions, users or other segmentation.

Sending executable logic to be executed runtime on the mobile app is treading on thin ice. Apple prohibited all forms of native executable code up until 2017, after when they softened this policy for developer tools. Sending JavaScript code from the backend to the mobile app is currently allowed, but only in cases that do not substantially change how your application works. However, Apple could decide to change this policy in the future.

Sending over metadata that controls the mobile app's behavior is a more common approach. This solution is future-proof on iOS, even if Apple was to decide to ban Javascript executable code sent to apps. The idea is to create a shell that interprets the metadata and dynamically builds interfaces and functionality in the app. Apps like this still cannot get around the fact that the mobile shell can not be updated easily. The shell should contain no client-side business logic beyond interpreting backend instructions. Even for the v1 of this shell, you need to think several backend versions ahead.

The backend will need to be aware of different mobile versions, and ensure it sends compatible "messages" to each client. This leads to needing to decide how to handle versioning; when to make changes to an API, when to introduce a new API version, or when to create a new endpoint. Luckily, neither versioning nor building for backwards-compatibility are novel problems. Still, if you decide to build a mobile shell that interprets metadata, you will probably be up for a challenge.

At Uber, we built an in-house system similar to this, and learned the hard way to not ship hardcoded client-side logic in the shell code, on how to get versioning right, and how challenging testing of such a system can be. Lyft, Airbnb, Zalando, and many other companies have built their own backend-driven-UI approaches. You can read more on various approaches in this Mobile Native Foundation discussion.

Further reading:

- A one-year PWA retrospective from Pinterest
- Engineering a high performance web app for the global market from Uber
- Javascript manipulation on iOS using WebKit from Capital One
- Migrating to WKWebView from Lucidchart
- Pitfalls in Android Webview implementation from 1mg Technology
- Server-driven UI approach from Lyft
- Server-driven rendering from Airbnb
- Backend-driven UI strategy from Zalando
- Backend-driven UI strategies from the Mobile Native Foundation discussion boards

Resources for this chapter:
go.mobileatscale.com/29

PART V

CHALLENGES DUE TO STEPPING UP YOUR GAME

Your approach to mobile engineering changes when you are aiming to build not just a good enough mobile app, but a best-in-class experience. This change in approach might come as a result of your app serving millions of customers, or it can be because you want to make world-class mobile experiences part of your app's DNA from day one.

This part covers problems that "world-class" apps tackle from the early days. We will cover non-functional aspects like code quality, compliance, privacy, compliance. We will also go through experimentation and feature flag approaches that are table-stakes for innovative apps, and other areas you need to pay attention to, like performance, app size, or forced upgrading approaches.

Let's get started!

30

EXPERIMENTATION

Any company that has a mobile app that drives reasonable revenue will A/B tests even small changes. This approach allows for both measuring the impact for changes and ensuring there are no major regressions that impact customers — and revenue — negatively.

Feature flags are just the first necessary tool for an experimentation system. Controlled rollout via staging and user bucketing, analyzing the results, detecting and responding to regressions and post-experiment analysis all make up an advanced and powerful experimentation system.

When you are small, experimentation is easy enough, mostly because you rarely have more than a few experiments taking place. Compare this to an Uber-scale app, where there might be more than 1,000 experiments running at any given time, each experiment targeting different cities and target groups, and some experiments impacting each other.

Tooling is one part of the question. There are plenty of pretty mature experimentation systems out there — some built for native mobile — from the ground up.

In-house experimentation systems are common for larger companies for a few reasons:

- **Novel systems.** Many of these systems are novel, evolving as data science and engineering evolves within the company. There is often nothing as advanced on the market as the data science team wants.
- **Data sources** can come from many places, several of which are in-house. For example, you can directly link an experiment with revenue generated, and compare that to the treatment group's revenue.
- **Supporting many teams** in an efficient way is not something most third-party experimentation platforms do well.
- **Data ownership** is clear: all experiment data stays in-house.
- **Core capabilities** for tech companies are rarely "outsourced". As of today, the ability to rapidly experiment and make decisions based on data is large enough of an advantage to want to keep it in-house. Even if it means spending more money, an in-house solution can allow the company to stay ahead of the competition.

Even if there was an alternative solution that a company could buy, it would mean an expensive migration, and some in-house features might work differently, or not even exist. For example, Uber had unique regulatory requirements for certain cities and regions that had to be baked into how experiments were or were not rolled out to a certain region. This regulatory requirement was specific to the gig economy and to specific cities. It is highly unlikely that any experimentation platform on the market would know the context to be able to support that use case.

Companies which chose to keep experimentation in-house include Uber, Amazon, Google, Netflix, Twitter, Airbnb, Facebook, Door-dash, LinkedIn, Dropbox, Spotify, Adobe, Oracle, Pinterest, Skyscanner, Prezi, and many others. Skyscanner is an example of a company who started with a vendor — Optimizely — before deciding to move experimentation in-house.

Motivations for moving to a vendor from in-house solutions are often cost-based (it is more expensive to operate and maintain the current system than using a vendor is), and standardization (having a unified platform instead of several teams building and maintaining custom tooling, and doing experiments in silos). GoDaddy is an example where they moved part of their experimentation to a vendor solution, in an effort to standardize across orgs, while keeping the feature flag implementation in-house.

Off-the-shelf experimentation and feature flag systems are plenty, and small to middle-sized companies and teams typically choose one of them. This is the point where building, operating and maintaining an in-house system could be more expensive and come with fewer features, than does choosing a vendor.

Popular vendor choices include Firebase Remote Config, Lauch-Darkly, Optimizely, Split.io and others. On top of a feature flagging system, many companies use a product analytics framework for more advanced analysis, Amplitude being a commonly quoted one.

The other difficulty is process; keeping track of experiments, and making sure they do not impact each other. For a small team, this is not a big deal. But when you have more than a dozen teams experimenting, you will encounter experiments impacting each other.

Process and tooling can both help with keeping track of experiments. Broadcasting upcoming experiments, data scientists or product managers syncing and a tool that makes it easy to locate and monitor active experiments can all help here. Most of these will be things you need to put in place as custom within the company, though.

Experimenting with every change is a common approach at companies with large apps, where the business impact of a change gone wrong could be bad. Uber is a good example where every mobile change needed to be reversible, and behind a feature flag. Even in the case of bug fixes, the fix would be put behind a feature flag, and rolled out as an A/B test. We would monitor key business metrics such as signup completion, trip taking rate or payments success rate, and keep track of any regression. All changes in the app needed to not reduce the key business metrics.

Was this approach an overkill? For a small application, it would be. However, at Uber, this approach helped us catch problems that resulted in people taking fewer trips. Even a 1% decline in trips would be measured in the hundreds of millions dollars per year, so there was reason to pay attention to this.

I recall shipping a bug fix to address the issue that when topping up a digital wallet, users saw an error when trying to top up over the allowed limit of, say $50. We made a fix so that whenever you entered an amount larger than this number, the textbox would correct itself to the maximum amount of $50. We tested the fix, then started to roll out.

On rollout, we saw a statistically significant drop on top ups happening, so we rolled back. It turned out that people wanting to top up larger amounts were being confused about what was happening when they entered a sum larger than $50, and they abandoned topping up. Had it not been for experimenting, we would have missed the fact that the fix actually caused a regression.

The question of who owns experiments, and coordinating them, is something that should be clarified at the team-level. The most common setup is for either data scientists, or for PMs to own experimentation, working with engineering to make sure the experiment is implemented correctly. However, engineers rarely own the rollout of the control / treatment groups, or decide on how to bucket users.

Further reading on experimentation, much of this is not only applicable to mobile:

- Building an intelligent experimentation platform, analyzing

experiment outcomes and a Bring your own metrics
platform from Uber
- Experimentation analysis platform from Doordash
- Our new experimentation platform from Spotify
- Our experimentation engine from LinkedIn
- Our experimentation platform, part 1 from Zalando
- Scaling our experimentation platform from Airbnb
- It's about A/B testing: our experimentation platform from Netflix
- Scalable feature toggles and A/B testing from Grab
- Wasabi: an open source A/B testing platform from Intuit
- Building our A/B testing platform from Pinterest
- Experimentation: technical overview from Twitter
- A/B testing mobile apps on iOS from Farfetch
- Building a Culture of Experimentation from Harvard Business Review

Resources for this chapter:
go.mobileatscale.com/30

31

FEATURE FLAG HELL

Everyone who has used feature flags will tell you that they are great. I agree with how much more confidence — and data — using these will give you. However, over time, the downsides of feature flags become apparent.

Using a typical feature flag typically looks similar to this in the codebase:

```
if (featureFlagActive) {
    // New functionality
} else {
    // Original functionality
}
```

Adding new functionality with a feature flag helps with a few things:

- **A/B testing and experimentation**. When building new functionality, the team assumes that it will do better than what was there before. Using feature flags allows you to A/B test this approach, to gather data and confirm this hypothesis. After the A/B test is complete, you would fully roll out the feature flag.

- **Gradual rollout**. Even after you test that the experiment works as expected, you often do not want to roll out the change, all at once. Gradual feature rollouts are common for apps with a large user base. The team usually monitors that metrics look as expected, and there is no unexpected uptick in user issues related to the new feature.
- **Regional rollouts**. Some features are meant to only be rolled out to certain regions or specific user groups. Feature flags make these rollouts easy to administer.

Feature problems become more common as the number of active feature flags in an application grows. This is usually parallel to the development team and the app complexity, increasing.

Feature flags which are dependent on one another is an interesting edge case that can happen with complex rollouts. Take the example of SubFeature being built within MainFeature. The team building SubFeature might want to treat 50% of users of the user population and roll out the flag accordingly. However, only users who are treated to MainFeature would see SubFeature, and if MainFeature is not rolled out to 100% of users, SubFeature would be seen by far fewer users than the team expects.

Mapping out feature flags dependencies as part of rollout plans is how most teams solve this problem. Though this issue might not seem like a complex one, I have observed teams working on complex apps running into the same issue time after time.

Conflicting feature flags become an issue as the development team grows. Take two teams; TeamA and TeamB building their respective features, behind FlagA and FlagB. They both test that this feature works when their flag is turned on. However, they are unaware of the other team building their feature and so do not test it with that flag switched on. During rollout, when both FlagA and FlagB are turned on, a part of the app breaks.

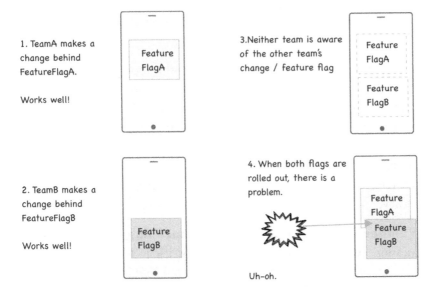

1. TeamA makes a change behind FeatureFlagA.

Works well!

Feature FlagA

2. TeamB makes a change behind FeatureFlagB

Works well!

Feature FlagB

3.Neither team is aware of the other team's change / feature flag

Feature FlagA

Feature FlagB

4. When both flags are rolled out, there is a problem.

Uh-oh.

Feature FlagA

Feature FlagB

Conflicting feature flags in a mobile app

Feature flags growing stale in the codebase become a serious problem after a while. These stale feature flags are either treated, or were never rolled out. Either way, there is now dead code in the app.

I believe that stale feature flags are worse than dead code. With dead code on the backend or the web, you can confirm pretty quickly that the code is dead. If you accidentally delete living code and deploy, you can undo this mistake by re-adding the code and deploying again.

With mobile, there is a very real danger of deleting non-dead code behind a feature flag. So mobile codebases end up being littered with if-else expressions referencing the feature flags. Many of these expressions stay in the codebase indefinitely, impacting both read-ability, maintainability, and — to a small extent — binary size.

The best way to clean up flags is to automate this work as much as possible. After a feature flag is rolled out fully, create an automated pull request that removes the dead execution path and the flag. This is the idea behind the Piranha tool built and open-sourced at Uber.

Once this tool was in place, we started to remove old feature flags with more confidence and faster.

A criticism of a tool like Piranha is that the tool is only as good as the codebase allows it. Piranha will not work well on codebases that have inconsistent coding styles around feature flags. When encountering code that is written in a different style, it can also make suggestions that could cause outages. Introducing a tool like Piranha works better when feature flags follow a consistent coding pattern enforced by a linter, or use a shared and opinionated feature flag library.

Whether to build your custom feature flagging system is a question every team needs to answer for itself. There are plenty of mature vendor solutions on the market that integrate well with iOS and Android and allow granular targeting for feature flags.

Building your own feature flagging system is a massive undertaking and the mobile components are the smaller part of it. The flag rollout system and setting it up to support experimentation, is a larger part of the work. At Uber, we had our own system built into our experimentation platform and integrated with multiple in-house solutions. I would not recommend this approach unless you have a solid business case and you have confirmed that using vendors does not make sense.

However, building a facade on top of vendor feature flags solutions can be a smart solution. This is what JustEat has done with the open-sourced JustTweak component on iOS. This facade allows them to switch, and fallback to, various feature flag providers.

Further reading:

- Piranha: an open source tool to automatically delete stale code from Uber
- A smart feature flagging system for iOS from Just Eat
- Using feature flags for mobile apps from VMWare
- Our journey of feature flag development from LINE
- Remote feature flags don't always come for free from ProAndroidDev

Resources for this chapter:
go.mobileatscale.com/31

32

PERFORMANCE

Mobile app performance is something you rarely need to worry about with small apps and something that becomes increasingly important, as your app — and the mobile team working on the app — grows. Google penalizes apps with poor performance metrics, ranking them lower on the Google Play store rankings. Users will eventually abandon problematic apps, according to a 2015 Techbeacon study. Since the study, expectations for "snappy" apps have likely only increased.

Common real-world performance bottlenecks with large apps:

- **App startup time bloating**, after several teams add "just one small thing" that needs to be done at startup. This could be a network request, or a small operation that blocks the CPU. At Uber, the Mobile Platform team took ownership of app startup time. This meant debugging why the app took so long and working around the issues, for example, by combining network requests. The team also put in place app startup measurements to detect any regression on app startup and to investigate when this happened.

- **Too many parallel networking calls**. Several components might be making independent networking requests at the same time, impacting networking performance. As the number of teams consuming networking grows, a common solution is to have a platform team own the networking layer. This team typically starts measuring the impact of parallel resources, and might put in place a priority system for calls, where they limit the number of parallel requests. Optimizing networking will be heavily dependent on what the app does, and how important low latency networking is.

- **Networking performance**, especially with low bandwidth or high latency cases. For apps that are used by tens or hundreds of millions of users, a growing number of these users will be using the app with poor connectivity. In some cases, using a different protocol than HTTP/2 could be an answer. This is the approach Uber came up with, using QUIC, a protocol over UDP. You can look to other protocols as well; the healthcare app Halodoc uses MQTT as their network layer.

- **Battery consumption rate.** The more teams work on the app, the more space there is for unnecessary CPU usage to happen, both while running the app, or when in the background. The early Skype apps were infamous for draining the battery and this characteristic led to higher user churn. Profiling CPU performance, and sampling to see the worst offenders are all good strategies to reduce resource usage. A dedicated mobile platform team owning battery consumption typically helps move the needle more than if each team is left to optimize their part of the stack.

- **Application not responding** (ANR) occurs when the UI thread is blocked for too long in an application. Users notice the app does not respond, and will have to kill the app, or on Android, the OS will offer to kill the process.

You want to both avoid the app getting in this state, but also detect and fix when it does.

- **Frozen frames and slow rendering frames** indicate the app is being slow, and seemingly unresponsive. Slow rendering frames refer to more than 0.1% of frames taking 700ms to render, while frozen frames refer to UI frames where it takes more than 16ms to render for 50% or more of frames. These or similar metrics help measure if the app can feel "very slow" for some users, or "jerky" for others.

- **Animations & UI rendering performance** is another visible issue, especially with custom animations and UI elements, on older devices. Tracing and profiling is the usual way to go about debugging issues, as well as keeping an eye out for slow rendering frames or frozen frames. Tools that help with debugging UIs include Reveal for iOS and Layout Inspector for Android. One of the problems with profiling is how the iOS and Android tracing instrumentation add overheads that result in animations and key transitions running slower under these conditions, and make investigations harder. Uber built and open-sourced Nanoscope in order to trace with less overhead and debug animation issues with more accuracy.

Measuring and improving the performance on a per-screen basis is a common approach when building most apps. Wayfair wrote a good summary on their approach, with a before-and-after video. The root cause of a page being slow is frequently not a mobile-only concern, but a combination of how the mobile app and the backend work together.

Once you see a visible performance issue such as a screen being "slow", the easiest way to debug performance issues is by starting from the mobile client. Measure how long each function takes by profiling or tracing, and then divide and conquer. See which calls are redundant on mobile clients, and see where you need to improve the performance for the backend endpoints.

Manually profiling your application is something you can easily get started with by using Instruments on iOS and Android Profiler with Android studio. While it is a great way to start, unfortunately, manually profiling apps will not scale well. You will have trouble getting "real data", especially when your app is used by a large number of users on a variety of devices. In this case, both the hardware variety and usage patterns can be ones that you cannot simulate with manual profiling.

Automating profiling of apps would in theory be a good step towards measuring performance characteristics, and spotting performance regressions. Unfortunately, automating the performance measurement process is complicated. To do so, you need to write and maintain a good number of automated UI or end-to-end tests. Once you do this, you need to automate performance profiling. Automating Instruments is a challenging task; the PSPDFkit team could not find a workaround to do so.

Even if you were able to automate the performance profiling of these tests, you would still only get a fraction of the "real world" data. Your results might show that the app runs fast enough on an emulator or your test devices, but what about users who have older devices or OS versions?

Sampling real-world app performance measurements is a far more reliable and scalable solution to keeping the performance characteristics of your app in-check. At Uber, we built an in-house solution to measure the latency of screens, networking, and functions within the app, and to report it to the backend. We segmented the data based on newer and older devices and alerted teams whose code and functions were performing poorly. Here is what a reporting dashboard looked like:

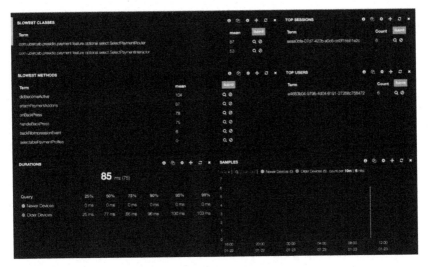

Visualizing real-world app performance at Uber through sampled data.

Doing any sort of sampling, or tracing, will have an impact on the performance of the code, so it is not wise to ship this to the majority of production users. A better approach is to enable such sampling for beta users, and optionally measure a small sample size of production users.

Networking performance is an area that can get tricky to stay on top of. You want your app to keep working well with poor networking conditions. A few ideas on how you can keep good "networking hygiene" as an area of focus for the wider team:

- **Artificially reducing the network speed** is something we did at Uber. For a few months, every Thursday, the networking layer in the beta app would slow traffic for employees to attempt to emulate low bandwidth conditions, and raise awareness of low bandwidth use cases. The experiment was a success, with engineers making several improvements that would have probably not happened without this nudge.
- **Dropping some network requests and injecting latency** is how the team at Wave raises awareness for real-world network scenarios. They drop 10% of the network

requests on development builds and add latency at the networking layer. This approach reminds people to minimize roundtrips, to build good "loading" UIs and to make every mutation idempotent.

Performance characteristics worth measuring, either as manual profile run, automated ones, or sampling real-world usage.

- **App startup time** and tracking how app startup changes, as the application grows.
- **Latency of loading screens**, identifying screens that are the slowest, and code that contributes most to this delay.
- **Networking performance:** measured as latency and parallel requests occurring on the client-side, and as error rate by endpoint.
- **Memory consumption**: measured by the memory used by the app, or simply by the device's free memory.
- **Local store size**, if the app uses local storage. For example, when caching locally to ensure cache eviction policy works properly.
- **UI performance**, for example, by measuring dropped frames, slow frames or frozen frames.
- **Automate measuring performance characteristics** as much as you can. Automated profiling, sampling real-world performance data, or monitoring non-functional metrics similar to how Halodoc has done so are all good approaches.

Using a p95 measurement point is a sensible choice for mobile because this will give you the number that most people experience, not counting the slowest 5%, which will likely include people on slow devices or with well below average connectivity. As your app grows to serve hundreds of millions of people, you might consider moving this up to p99, to ensure that almost everyone using the app has a good experience, even on old devices and with poor connections.

Performance: APMs vs Automated Testing

Leland Takamine, one of the creators of Nanoscope and the cofounder of perf.dev shares his take on whether to monitor performance, or execute automated tests for measurements.

APM Origins

Application Performance Monitoring (APM) is a borrowed concept from server-side development. The idea is this: Monitor end-user metrics in production and sound the alarm if your users experience any performance degradation. Entire industries have been built around this strategy for backend development (Datadog, New Relic, Dynatrace), so it is no surprise that mobile companies have adopted similar tactics. Crashlytics, one of the first Android APMs, was founded in 2011.

Today, the market is saturated with APM solutions that aim to make Mobile production monitoring easier and smarter. But what mobile companies are beginning to realize is that production monitoring is proving to be far less useful on mobile than it has been on the backend.

Why APMs Do Not Cut It on Mobile

When your backend APM identifies a problem in production, you can simply roll back the latest deployment. The issue is resolved in a matter of minutes. On mobile, there is no such rollback mechanism. Your users are stuck with any production issues until your next release, which typically takes a minimum of two weeks to roll out. Even worse, you may not be able to root cause the issue at all, based on production data. Meanwhile, you are losing users because of the poor experience.

This long feedback loop renders production monitoring — a reactive strategy that worked well for backed development — much less effective on mobile.

Automated Performance Testing

So what is the fix? Be proactive instead of reactive. Leading mobile companies are now looking towards automated testing solutions to catch performance issues in CI before releasing to users. It seems obvious given the ubiquity of functional testing, but performance benchmarking is a different beast. Degradation happens slowly over many code changes, and the noise in your performance benchmarks will likely mask any small regressions in CI. This is precisely the challenge companies face when building in-house performance testing solutions.

Traditional CI infrastructure and device farms do not provide the necessary level of consistency, which is why mobile teams are turning to third parties which specialize in providing consistent performance testing infrastructure. Perf.dev is leading the charge in this space and is a smart choice for any company looking to proactively address and avoid mobile performance problems. To learn more, visit perf.dev or reach out at hello@perf.dev.

You Should Be Doing Both

Even though APMs are not ideal for mitigating performance problems, they are useful for keeping a pulse on end-user app performance. You always want to know where you stand in terms of performance in the real world. But remember to avoid relying on APMs to catch specific performance problems because- you will not be able to react quickly enough. For improving and maintaining excellent mobile performance, automated performance testing and debugging tooling are your best friends.

———

Performance monitoring tools:

- Nanoscope: an extremely accurate method tracing tool for Android, from Uber.
- Profilo: understand Android app performance in the wild, from Facebook.
- Firebase performance: monitor Android and iOS apps.
- perf.dev: application performance testing from the creators of Nanoscope.

Resources for further reading:

- App startup time guide from Google
- Building a blazingly fast Android app from LinkedIn
- Monitoring non-functional metrics from Halodoc
- Journey to a faster everyday super app from Grab
- Employing the QUIC protocol from Uber
- Optimizing the Netflix Android application from Netflix
- Building smooth Android animations and smooth iOS animations from Netflix
- MobileLab: preventing mobile performance regressions from Facebook
- Improving our iOS app performance from Skyscanner
- Our approach to monitoring iOS application performance from Mercari engineering

Resources for this chapter:
go.mobileatscale.com/32

33

ANALYTICS, MONITORING AND ALERTING

Monitoring and alerting for things going wrong is common practice on backend and web teams. A spike in 5xx responses, or an increase in exceptions often raises an alarm, pages the team, and engineers mitigate the root cause.

For mobile apps, crash reporting is a similar approach. App crashes are the most obvious and impactful things that can go wrong. Mobile teams typically have set up crash reporting and alerting solutions, either using vendors like Bugsnag, or building homegrown tools.

However, business monitoring and business events alerting is often a distant second thought in the app development lifecycle in my experience. Monitoring mobile apps can and should run deeper than just monitoring for crashes. Mature teams detect when there are regressions in a critical flow, get an alert, and start investigating what the root cause might be.

Mobile Analytics

The first step in monitoring for business events is to decide what we want to measure. What flows and metrics matter for a given mobile feature?

The analytics tool to log and analyze the data is one where you can choose vendor solutions, or go in-house:

- **Google Analytics** wrapped with the Firebase Analytics SDK is a popular way to get started: it is free, and a good enough start for most teams.
- **Other vendor** offerings such as Amplitude, Flurry, Mixpanel, Fullstory, Appsee and others all offer various capabilities. From this group, Amplitude stands out as one of the most advanced products analytics suites on the market.
- **In-house analytics** is something large organizations with available resources take on. Cost is the largest drawback, while customization, building features that vendors do not provide, integrating with in-house data sources and data ownership are reasons why companies sometimes go ahead with this approach. At Uber, we used in-house analytics due the scale of the data, and the in-house tooling we were able to use this way.

iOS and Android events and flows being different is a major pain point for any analytics approach. Ideally, you want to visualize flows across iOS and Android. However, in practice, it often means lots of work to manually "match up" events on both platforms, especially if iOS and Android teams work in silos.

Teams that take analytics seriously will often consider events in the planning phase, coordinate with the other platform, and work with product and data science to ensure they emit enough data for efficient tracking.

Business Events Monitoring

Getting raw mobile analytics, such as screens displayed or user actions made, is the first step in the monitoring journey. Mapping events that the business actually cares about is the next one.

First, you need to define the critical business events and paths in the app. At Uber, we did this with product managers and data scientists. For example, on Payments, we came up with the following key business events:

- A new user adds their first payment instrument on sign up
- An existing user adds a new payment instrument
- A user updates their payment
- A user tops up a wallet from within the app
- A user deletes a payment method
- An error occurs when attempting to use a payment method

The next step is implementing cross-platform monitoring for the business events. At Uber, this meant creating real-time graphs that charted all of these business events, cross-platform. We had to map iOS and Android events separately for their respective flows, as the two codebases were separate, and then ensure that analytics updates did not break the mapping.

Being able to drill down to regions or sub-features is a typical need for large apps. At Uber, we needed to be able to narrow our monitoring all the way to the city level, as we would often launch experiments starting with a single city or country.

Metrics being wrong, but no one in the company noticing for months or years is far more of a common problem than most teams or companies realize. Measuring Daily Active Users incorrectly across iOS, Android and mobile web is a good example, as explained in the talk When Metrics Lie by Pinterest mobile engineering manager Ryan Cooke at Droidcon SF 2018.

I have observed companies over-estimating native web and underestimating native mobile retention or user activity. The same companies then incorrectly allocated millions of dollars in marketing budget to a channel that in reality, did not perform as well as the numbers showed. It always came down to one issue, that analytics were implemented slightly differently on iOS, Android and on mobile web.

Certifying metrics is a process that Pinterest has been doing for years with good success. Certified metrics require a clear product specification (spec), ensuring consistent implementation. A product spec means a consistent definition, considered edge cases and helps understand stakeholder needs. The Pinterest team found inconsistent implementations caused more harm than good and introduced this certification process.

Certification Process

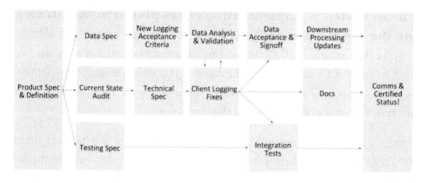

The metrics certification process at Pinterest.

Data verification on top of certified metrics is where Pinterest has seen the biggest success. They use three steps:

1. **Anomaly detection** such as alerting when seeing week-over-week oddities. This approach is the most trivial to implement and it catches some regressions.
2. **Deep diving into the data and comparing it with**

other data points. For example, when comparing active users with users who are seeing content. If certain users are shown content but are not considered active users, there is a problem that needs to be identified. This is the approach that uncovered a large chunk of the issues.

3. **Validating metrics logged correctly** with automated UI tests, to confirm the logging that the server receives, works as expected. These tests are expensive to write and maintain. However, without these in place, there is no way to reliably detect metrics regressions. Pinterest found these tests to catch the majority of metrics issues, before they make it into production.

You need to monitor your metrics behaving correctly beyond just the initial implementation. One of the common ways metrics go wrong is after a change is made to a previously correct implementation, and having no monitoring to detect this degradation.

Mobile Alerting

How do you detect if there is a suspicious change in one of the business events that is connected to the mobile app? To do so, you need to put automated alerting in-place.

Should mobile engineers be paged if something looks suspicious with the mobile business events? Every team will have to come up with its own answer to this. What is the impact of not noticing drops in critical business metrics?

Real-time mobile alerts are not the norm in the industry. In a non-representative Twitter poll with 168 responses, a quarter of mobile engineers said they have real-time mobile alerts in place:

Do You Have Real-Time Mobile Alerts In-Place?

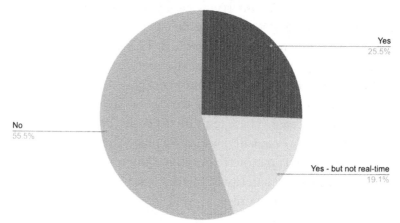

Yes
25.5%

No
55.5%

Yes - but not real-time
19.1%

The majority of mobile engineering teams probably do not have real-time
mobile alerts in place.

Crash report alerting is the most common type of alerting
teams have in place. Several vendor solutions make it easy to
configure crash spikes to trigger PagerDuty or other integrations.
For example, Bugsnag offers configurable crash alerts with their
Alerting and Workflow Engine.

In-house implementation for crash alerting is often done to support
catching regressions on the release and beta builds. Be warned
though that grouping crashes and detecting patterns (e.g. crashes
only occurring on certain devices) becomes more challenging than
many people expect.

Rollout alerting on health metrics is something you can put in
place when you have good enough business events monitoring. You
can then monitor any regression for the key business metrics. At
Uber, metrics we could not afford to degrade were related to people
taking trips. At every build train step, we would monitor, visualize
and alert on regressions for related events, monitoring at a regional
level.

Rollout monitoring and alerting on key health metrics at Uber,
at a regional level.

Alerting on business event changes is something far fewer mobile teams do, even when building large and widely-used apps. The teams which do this tend to build on top of alerting tools that are not specific to mobile. For example, Uber sent mobile events to an in-house anomaly detection service, and received alerts when this service determined something strange was going on. The Twitch team used Cloudwatch anomaly detection for mobile events on top of their Kinesis events streaming.

Noise for mobile business events will be the biggest issue you face if you start alerting on these events. Apps have cyclical usage, and these cycles will be different in various regions. Real-world events can cause a surge or a decrease in mobile app usage, which then can trigger anomaly detection. At Uber, in the early days, the mobile teams were regularly paged after concerts and local promotions that caused an unusual spike in app usage, until we relaxed thresholds on these alerts to deliberately make them less sensitive.

Regional alerting for a number of app features becomes an even more challenging problem, if you want to do it on the mobile side. At Uber, we supported more than10 payment methods across close to 60 countries, and wanted to get notified if any payment method had anomalies in any country. The reason we needed this granularity is that it took us months to detect that PayPal was not working in Japan.

For this type of alerting, you almost certainly need to build in-house solutions. At Uber, our first challenge in setting up this alerting was with data cardinality, the multiple dimensions of data we needed to store and alert on. Once we managed to store and analyze the data, sparse data sets became problematic; in some countries, certain payment methods were barely used. It took us months of tweaking to get our alerting to the level we wanted. However, once we did, we detected regional payment provider outages just as fast — and sometimes faster — than the payment providers themselves.

Further reading:

- Mobile analytics guide from Amplitude
- M3: an open source, large-scale metrics platform for Prometheus from Uber
- Real-time anomaly detection from Uber
- When Metrics Lie from Pinterest engineering manager Ryan Cooke
- Monitoring business performance data with ThirdEye smart alerts from LinkedIn
- Getting started with behavioural analytics from Amplitude
- Non-functional metrics monitoring in Android from Halodoc
- Providing accurate iOS analytics data from Tokopedia engineering
- Driving data-driven decisions from Spotify
- How the fastest growing game in the App Store retains its users from QuizUp

Resources for this chapter:
go.mobileatscale.com/33

34

MOBILE ONCALL

Having a mobile on-call rotation will become a sensitive topic, once you have mobile alerts in place, even if these alerts are just for crash reporting. When an alert fires, it needs to page someone who knows how to mitigate this outage. The obvious choice is a mobile engineer who has all the necessary context.

If you have a large enough mobile team, having a mobile-only on-call might not be a problem. At Uber, on the Payments teams we followed this setup for a few years. The primary and secondary on-calls were always a pair of iOS and Android engineers, or engineers familiar with both the codebases.

Keeping a (very) small mobile on-call rotation is what many teams end up with, though. This is because mobile on-call is almost always quiet, save for a few crash reports. So even with a small rotation, being on the rotation should not mean much stress. Still, I am always wary of any on-call rotation with fewer than five engineers. What happens if something blows up, but the on-call is not around?

Having on-call rotation is only the first step to dealing with outages. There also needs to be a clear incident response procedure, and the engineers who go on-call need to be trained for it, so they know what to do when they get paged.

A common incident response starts with the on-call engineers assessing the severity of the issue and the number of customers impacted. Next, they decide if the incident needs to be escalated. If so, they might involve others and decide who is leading the response. For larger incidents, they might need to divide and conquer on who is leading a conference call with others, who is handling communications with stakeholders, and who is investigating certain parts of the issue. It takes time and practice to build good incident response muscles within an on-call team. It is an investment you need to make if you want to increase your response times, minimize mitigation times and the impact upon customers.

The organization needs to learn from incidents, to ensure that the app will not break twice due to the same root cause. Having a postmortem process is key for these learnings.

Postmortems are a tool to capture details of the incident, such as its context, timeline, business impact, root cause, and corrective actions. Postmortems should include follow-up actions to improve systems and processes, so a similar outage will be prevented, or at least detected and mitigated more quickly next time. Reading postmortems of other teams is a great way to share learnings across the company.

Merging backend and mobile on-calls will become tempting on product teams where you do not have enough mobile engineers to warrant a mobile-only on-call. However, you will likely find that the backend engineers might not be thrilled about the idea, and the mobile engineers even less so. The reason? They are both unsure what to do when an alert comes in.

A good on-call is one where engineers do not need to think too much about what to do when an alert comes in. There should be few, simple steps to take and ideally these steps are part of an on-call runbook.

Does your on-call have runbooks for most alerts? Are they simple enough to follow?

If the answer is yes, congratulations! You are ready to merge mobile and backend on-calls. People will go on-call less frequently, and both mobile and backend engineers will understand the product better, over time.

If you do not have enough runbooks, or they are not good enough; why not? Not having good runbooks means the team relies more on the experienced engineers to help with on-call, who are seen to have it "all in their head". New joiners take much longer to go on-call. And just as importantly, mobile engineers cannot go on-call for backend alerts, or vice versa. So what will it be; keep a stressful on-call, hire more people, or get the runbooks in order?

As further reading, I recommend going through the Being On-call chapter in the Site Reliability Workbook from Google.

Resources for this chapter:
go.mobileatscale.com/34

35

ADVANCED CODE QUALITY CHECKS

The shorter the feedback cycle between detecting issues with your code, the more productive both engineers and teams will be. While getting feedback on your code at code review is great, would it not be even better to get instant feedback, even before you submit your code to code review?

Productive teams put advanced code checking infrastructure in place early on, exactly to help with rapid feedback on easy-to-spot code quality issues. Linting and static analysis are the two most common approaches and are often used together.

Code formatting is one of the most common use cases of code quality checks. The code formatter would be run before creating a pull request, ensuring that all code up for review follows the style guide that the team agreed on and defined in the formatter. Popular code formatters include SwiftFormat or Google-java-format.

———

SonarSource static analysis tools support Swift, Objective-C, Kotlin & Java along with several additional languages. Tight integration with GitHub, GitLab, Azure DevOps & Bitbucket means easy adoption within your team workflow regardless of where you keep your code.

Used by more than 200,000 engineering teams - start analyzing your code quality and code security today:

- **SonarQube** is the on-premise code quality and code security tool. Get started for free at SonarQube.org.
- **SonarCloud** is the cloud-based code quality and security tool. Get started for free at SonarCloud.io.

———

Linting is a special case of static analysis; scanning the code for potential errors, beyond just code formatting. This can be as trivial as checks ensuring that indentation is correct, through enforcing naming patterns, all the way to more advanced rules such as declaring variables in alphabetical order. Popular linting tools include:

- iOS: the Clang analyzer — shipping with Xcode — and SwiftLint.
- Android: the lint tool — shipping with Android Studio — and ktlint for Kotlin.

As the team grows, it can make sense to start enforcing more complex rules across the codebase. These rules could be enforcing team-wide coding patterns, such as restricting forced values, or enforcing architecture "rules", such as a View not being allowed to invoke Interactors directly.

At Uber, we saw lots of value in adding architecture definitions as "lint enforceable" rules. To do so, the team built and open-sourced NEAL (Not Exactly A Linter) for more advanced pattern detection, used across iOS and Android.

Lint fatigue is a problem that starts to occur at large projects, or ones with many linting rules. As the errors or warnings pile up, engineers often start to ignore them. A good example is ignoring deprecation warnings when it is not clear how to migrate to a new implementation of an API.

A common way of dealing with lint fatigue is to make linting errors break the build, leaving no choice but to fix them. It is a bit annoying, but effective. Another approach is to build tools to fix linting errors automatically. This is an approach Instagram took; they used automated refactoring to educate engineers about coding best practices.

Static analysis is the more generic phrase of automatic inspection of the code, looking for potential issues and errors. Mobile static analysis tools usually help to detect use cases that are more complex than what a simple lint rule could catch.

Most static analysis tools are written for a language — Swift, Kotlin, Objective C, or Java — and detect common programming issues such as unused variables, empty catch blocks, possible null values, and others. On top of the linting tools listed above, static analysis tools you could consider are:

- Swift, Kotlin, Objective-C and Java: SonarQube and SonarCloud (advanced static analysis), NEAL, Infer (Java, Objective-C)
- Swift: Clang analyzer (ships with Xcode), SwiftLint, SwiftInfo, Tailor, SwiftFormat
- Kotlin: ktlint (a "no-decision" linter), detekt (code smells and complexity reports)
- Objective-C: Clang analyzer (ships with Xcode), OCLint
- Java: lint (ships with Android Studio), NullAway

(annotation-based null-checks), FlowDroid (data flow analysis), CogniCrypt (secure cryptography integration checks) PMD (Programming Mistake Detector), Checkstyle
- See also this repository of static analysis tools per language

The upside of using linting and static analysis tools is getting more rapid feedback and code reviewers not needing to check for the common code issues. Code quality generally stays higher with the tools enforcing rules. When using advanced tooling, static analysis can result in more stable and secure apps by detecting edge cases ahead of time. A good example of added stability is using a tool to prevent runtime crashes due to null objects and doing this by analyzing the code, compile-time.

The downside of these tools is the time it takes to integrate them and the additional maintenance they bring. You need to decide which tool to use and add them to your build setup, both to local builds and the CI/CD setup. Once in place, you might need to keep the rules up to date, and every now and then, update the version of the tool to support new features you might need.

The more complex tooling you choose, the more this maintenance might add up. At Uber, we set up extensive linting and static analytic checks. The outcome felt to me like it was worth the added effort. However, I would be hesitant to build the type of custom tooling we did, and instead would use a good enough tool for the job that can be set up with little effort.

Code coverage—checking which parts of your code are tested via unit tests, or other automated tests—is another tool to help with quality. For iOS, Xcode has built-in code coverage reports. For Android, Jacoco is a commonly used coverage reporting tool for Java and Kotlin. Several vendors also offer code coverage solutions. By integrating code coverage with your development workflow and CI setup, you can:

- Visualize how much coverage each change has. This can make it easy for engineers and code reviewers to verify if new business logic has been tested.
- Help enforce a minimum code coverage policy, if the team has agreed on an approach like this.
- Show code coverage trends over time. Do code coverage changes have any correlation with outages or other issues with the app? You will have the data to answer this question.
- Identify areas that are poorly covered, and where adding tests could help with correctness, maintainability and give more confidence to engineers making changes in those areas.

Further reading:

- Static analysis at scale from Instagram
- Kotlin linting with ktlint from Pinterest
- iOS linting tooling from Pinterest
- iOS: Continuous code inspection with SwiftLint & SwiftLint in Use
- Android: Android lint overview & Android lint framework - an introduction

Resources for this chapter:
go.mobileatscale.com/35

36

COMPLIANCE, PRIVACY AND SECURITY

There is a high likelihood that your app and your development process needs to adhere to certain compliance and privacy guidelines. The compliance requirements will be unique to each app. In this chapter, we will go through common ones.

Most larger mobile engineering teams work with a compliance team to determine which regulations, processes and guidelines they need to adhere to. Some companies have in-house compliance, privacy and security teams, while others hire external consultants. Compliance violations are costly, both upon reputation and also financially and you want to ensure your company takes this area seriously.

PII (Personally Identifiable Information) should not be accessible to anyone but those who should access these details. No mobile engineer, customer support folks, or people working at the company should be able to access this information.

GDPR (General Data Protection Regulation) is a significant piece of EU regulation which has further expanded the scope of PII. PII data can only be stored and processed when it has a lawful purpose.

Industry-specific compliance guidelines might apply to your app in certain industries. A non-exhaustive list of these includes:

- **PCI DSS** (Payment Card Industry Data Security Standard) compliance when handling credit card information.
- **HIPAA** (Health Insurance Portability and Accountability Act) and / or **ISO/IEC 27001** when working with healthcare-related data information.
- **FERPA** (Family Educational Rights and Privacy Act) for working with student or educational information in the US.
- **FCRA** (Fair Credit Reporting Act) for apps related to consumer reporting agencies such as credit companies, medical information companies or tenant screening.
- **Section 508** compliance test when working with US federal agencies, ensuring people with disabilities can access their electronic information technology (EIT).
- **European Accessibility Act** guidelines for when developing for a government within the EU.
- **Individual country privacy laws** that might apply to your app.

For mobile engineering, there are a couple of areas that will impact almost all organizations, except those with no users in the EU.

Logging of data both on the mobile and sending it over to the backend, is an area you should think more carefully about:

- **Logging PII data** without end-to-end encryption in place might invite data breaches.
- **Aim to not log PII data**, or instead anonymize this information in the logs, turning it into non-PII data.
- **Put guidance in place** for what, when, and how to log, including a section on PII data.
- **Audit logs** to ensure they are compliant with regulations you need to adhere to.
- **Bug report screenshots** should not contain PII data. You might need to do additional steps to ensure this is the

case, and information such as credit card numbers and
other PII information does not circulate in ticketing
systems, or at customer support agents.

- **Review** what data is being logged and how on a regular
basis to ensure there is no PII information being stored in a
non-secure way.

Audit various parts of your app for GDPR and PII
compliance.

- **Third-party SDKs**. These SDKs may often not be
GDPR-compliant by their default configuration. You might
need to work with their vendors and in some cases, stop
using some of them in order to stay compliant.
- **Mobile app workflows** might need to be updated to
ensure the app stays compliant with GDPR. This can
include additional steps to ask for permission for
activities, and could mean adding additional information
screens.
- **Mobile network traffic** is worth monitoring with tools
like mitmproxy, Charles, or similar others, to see what data
the app is sending through the network. You might discover
PII data being sent from your code or SDK code that you
need to resolve.

Training a few engineers on the implications of privacy laws for
coding and operations could be a smart investment. This way, you
bring some of this knowledge in-house instead of relying upon
external consultants. If your organization is large enough to have in-
house specialists, you might still want to consider nominating
compliance / privacy / security champions to better scale this
knowledge. This is what we did at Uber and it helped to flag potential issues earlier in the development process.

**Having a compliant development process and data
storage setup is out of the scope** for this book. To ensure both
your development processes, as well as your application and stored

data are compliant, you want to rely on security, legal, and compliance experts.

To give a sense of how much effort such a process would take, at Uber, we spent months mapping processes, making process and tool changes, and then auditing these as we prepared for GDPR to launch. The amount of work we had to do and the scale of the changes we made, made this project one of the bigger undertakings by the company.

The sooner you execute a thorough privacy and compliance review, the better. Once you have the right processes in place, staying compliant will be far less of an effort.

Secure mobile development is a continuously evolving topic. Though native iOS and Android mobile apps have fewer security challenges to worry about, it is a good idea to map potential vulnerabilities and to train engineers on secure mobile app development.

Running security checks at the CI/CD level means you can scan the code for hardcoded credentials or usage of dangerous functions. You can get this approach out of the box with tools like SonarCloud. Skyscanner took a similar approach with the Sonar Secrets plugin built on top of SonarQube, and their Whispers static code analysis tool. There are other vendor solutions that help with security or penetration testing.

At Uber, we had a separate mobile security training curriculum that included OWASP mobile security risks and MASVS (Mobile Application Security Verification Standard).

Further reading for compliance and privacy:

- Privacy and data protection in mobile applications from the EU cybersecurity agency
- Privacy design guidelines for mobile application development from IAPP

- What should software engineers know about GDPR from InfoQ
- 15 steps to developing GDPR-compliant apps from TechBeacon
- DHS Section 508 Compliance Test from US Homeland Security

For security:

- Mobile Application Security Verification Standard from OWASP
- Whispers: advanced secrets detection from Skyscanner
- Sonar Secrets: secrets detection on top of SonarQube from Skyscanner
- Driving Secure Software Development Lifecycle by adopting Mobile Security Analysis from Halodoc
- iOS and Android mobile app security best practices from Quickbird Studios
- OWASP Mobile Top 10 security risks from OWASP
- Android privacy and security from Google

Resources for this chapter:
go.mobileatscale.com/36

37

CLIENT-SIDE DATA MIGRATIONS

For mobile apps that store data locally, data schema changes in the app come with a new set of migration challenges.

This is an area that both backend and thick client engineers dealing with databases will be deeply familiar with. At the same time, this problematic space rarely exists with web apps, since web apps store little to no offline data in the browser, nor are they typically designed to support offline scenarios.

Migrations where you need to migrate on-device data from one format to another, is difficult. The bigger the data schema changes, the more effort such a migration entails. Writing a migrating function is the smaller part of this challenge. Other challenges include:

- **Testing the migration with real(ish) production data**, this data ideally represents so-called power users who have some of the most complex types of data stores on the device.
- **Testing upgrades from various old versions** to the new one. You cannot assume that people will update the

app from the last version. Assuming this is not the first such data migration, you might need to support a small number of users who are even one such migration behind.

- **Logging / alerting on the client side** for details of the data migration because backend logs might not be of much use for on-device data migrations.
- **Supporting customers** where data migration might have failed and having a backup plan, in case these users experience major functionality regressions.

A major challenge with schema migrations is what happens if the new version of the app has a bug which corrupts the new schema? Users of the app can be stuck in an invalid state, where the only option they have to recover, is to wipe the app and start from a clean state, as there is no rollback option on the client side.

Carefully consider if you can make the backend the source of truth in the case of data schema changes. Instead of having to build an error-prone, hard-to-debug, hard-to-support on-device schema migration, can you build support for re-downloading data from the backend — or make this an option for the future?

38

FORCED UPGRADING

In 2015, few apps had forced upgrading mechanisms in place. In 2021, most mature apps have put this in place, recognizing the need to force retire old versions of the app.

Reasons to implement forced upgrades are plentiful:

- **Retiring backend API versions**. Without forced upgrades in-place, backend APIs can not be retired.
- **Cost of testing**. Old app versions still need to be tested, especially against backend changes.
- **Customer support cost.** The more versions of an app are available, the more complicated — and costly — customer support will be. Even after fixing a known bug, users can still reach out to customer support reporting the same issue because they are using an older version.
- **Cost of backwards compatibility**. The backend team will have to move more carefully and ultimately, more slowly to ensure backwards compatibility for old app versions.
- **Severe bugs that need fixing**. There might be bugs that warrant immediate fixing, and immediate rollout of the fix.

Without a forced upgrade solution in place, ensuring all customers get the fix is not possible.

- **Vulnerabilities**. Old app versions might be exposed to security or other business vulnerabilities. If there is no way to force users to stop using these versions, the vulnerability cannot be patched.

Examples of forced upgrade implementations include:

- **Snapchat, Facebook Messenger and Whatsapp** all have a rolling window in place to not allow users to be using a version too far behind.
- **Games** frequently employ this strategy. When a new upgrade is rolled out, players often are not allowed to proceed without upgrading.
- **Banking** apps typically implement this approach. **Monzo** has support both for forced upgrades, as well as for recommended upgrades.
- **Just Eat** (a food delivery service in the UK) supports both skippable and forced upgrades. They target both on-demand or with a rolling window. The rolling window can be configured remotely. The company has had forced upgrading in place since 2013.
- **ITV Hub** (one of the top UK apps) has both a "soft" killswitch (asking the user to update) and a "hard" one, where it is mandatory to update. The killswitch can be rolled out based on OS version, app version, phone manufacturer and other targeting mechanisms.
- **Skyscanner** (air travel) uses a rolling window upgrade method.
- **Tresorit** (encrypted online storage) has built forced upgrades from the first public release of the app. In cryptography, it is critical to be able to switch to stronger algorithms and to not allow weak fallbacks after a grace period.

- **Halodoc** (healthcare) implements a mix of flexible and immediate app updates.

It is safe to say that all mature mobile apps do have some concept of forced upgrading in place and many of them have had this since day one.

The catch with forced upgrade is you need to build it much earlier than when you plan to use it. You can not safely retire app versions without a forced upgrade messaging mechanism in place.

This diagram shows the problem that first-time app developers face:

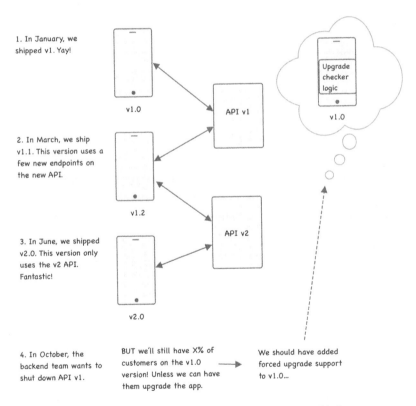

1. In January, we shipped v1. Yay!

v1.0

API v1

Upgrade checker logic

v1.0

2. In March, we ship v1.1. This version uses a few new endpoints on the new API.

v1.2

3. In June, we shipped v2.0. This version only uses the v2 API. Fantastic!

API v2

v2.0

4. In October, the backend team wants to shut down API v1.

BUT we'll still have X% of customers on the v1.0 version! Unless we can have them upgrade the app. ⟶ We should have added forced upgrade support to v1.0...

The challenge of forced upgrading: you should have built it well before you needed it.

Once a forced upgrade solution is in place, you do need to test it in production, to make sure it works. Some companies make the mistake of building forced upgrade support, but then not using it for years. When it is time for a forced upgrade, they will have little confidence in whether it will actually work.

On Android, Google offers in-app updates starting from Android 5.0 with an easy-to-use API. However, for older Android versions or for iOS, you are currently left with homegrown solutions.

How to support old phone models is a pain point you come across when using forced upgrades. While many businesses can decide to not support older phones, this is not always the case. An example is freight app Convoy, where some carriers have phones for which newer app versions using JS Core do not even work.

The decision on how to support these old models is something you need to decide based upon your business use case. Some apps end up supporting old app versions for years in order to keep these customers. Other apps draw a line after calculating the business value they get from a subset of users, and then communicate discontinuing support for certain OS versions for those customers.

Forced upgrade is not just a tool: it is a strategy. As you build the tool, make sure to work with the business — product managers and business stakeholders — to put the forced upgrade strategy in place. If you have the edge cases covered around when and how to force upgrade, this process will go from being a challenge to being a routine exercise.

39

APP SIZE

How much does app size matter? The larger the app, the less likely users are to download it, and the more likely they can remove it when their phone storage fills up.

Binary size is important, as it impacts downloads. The smaller the binary size, the more likely users will download the app. In 2017, Google reported a few interesting findings in the article Shrinking APKs, growing installs:

- **Every 6 MB increase in an APK's size saw a 1% decrease** in install conversion rates.
- **Download completion rate** was 30% higher for an APK with 10MB size, than for one with 100MB.
- **70% of people in emerging markets consider app size** before downloading the application.

There is no similarly thorough report for iOS, - but there is certainly some correlation between app size and install rates. For example, the Segment team observed a 66% drop in app installs when artificially inflating the size of an app from 3MB to 150MB in 2016.

For Android, keeping the binary as small as possible is especially important. Several devices have little storage, and in certain markets people decide whether to download an app based on the space it takes up.

One of the most straightforward ways to reduce the size of Android apps is packaging them as app bundles. This option has been available since late 2018. According to Google, the average app size is reduced by 35%, compared to universal APK packaging.

For iOS, the most important size-related constraint is the over-the-air download limit of 200MB. Apps larger than this can only be downloaded or updated over a wifi connection. At Uber, we artificially increased the app size for a release cycle to measure the impact of going over the OTA-limit. Uber found an enormous drop in installs that could have significantly impacted the business. Former Uber engineering manager Chris Brauchli dives deeper in the article Uber app's binary size woes.

Creating a separate, "Lite" app of a very small size is a strategy that companies such as Uber, Facebook and Google have taken for Android, in emerging markets. At Uber, research showed that in several markets potential customers were not downloading the relatively large app. This led to building and launching Uber Lite: a more limited Uber app, but one with a 5MB footprint, optimized for low bandwidth usage. Facebook Lite and Google Go are other apps that have been built with similar goals at mind.

To keep the app under 5MB and to reduce data usage, the team made several optimizations:

- **Maps turned off** by default to reduce data usage.
- **Removing frameworks** that added too large of an overhead. For example, Uber Lite does not use RIBs.
- **Using vector image formats** instead of PNGs for resources.
- **Server-driven client** where the backend does much of the orchestration to reduce network payloads.

- **Use a single TCP connection** by keeping request and response sizes under 1 MTU (maximum transmission unit).

Note that app size and bandwidth usage reduction frequently comes with tradeoffs. In the case of Uber Lite, these tradeoffs were:

- **More engineering effort** to maintain a small version of the app. A new team had to be set up to build and maintain this application.
- **More effort from the backend team** to support the low bandwidth use cases. The network calls had to be optimized to fit under 1 MTU, and some flows rethought completely.
- **Reduced functionality for customers** which can lead to lower conversion or less revenue per customer.

Ownership of the app binary size tends to be the trickiest question to resolve for growing organizations. With multiple teams working on the app, everyone tends to focus on building their own feature. Once there is a mobile platform team in place, this team typically takes ownership of both monitoring the app's size and coming up with ways to reduce it in a sensible way.

Static assets creeping into the binaries is a recurring problem with large-scale apps to which many teams contribute. You would be surprised how many apps out there embed a 6MB pristine JPEG file that was added for an A/B experiment, then the engineers forgot to remove it after the experiment. Having app size monitoring in place helps you catch these kinds of oversights. App size monitoring can prevent these unnecessary assets from reaching production and wasting space across a large number of devices.

If your company doesn't pay attention to the binary size, it might be time to change this approach. Even if it is not visible, a large app size will have some impact on installation and usage metrics. It is up to you to find out how large this impact could be, and how much time and effort you want to spend on optimizing the app size.

Installed size is also important, but few teams pay attention to tracking it. While an app might have a small enough binary size, this size can start increasing by caching things like images, files and other data. If the app grows too large, users might uninstall it and churn.

Google Play supports developers to view installed sizes through Google Play console and you should regularly monitor this data. Apple does not support doing so, meaning that for iOS, you will be left with manually checking how and when you cache, and testing locally on how your app's size changes.

Further reading:

- Reduce your app size on iOS by app thinning from Apple
- Shrink, obfuscate and optimize your Android app from Google
- The Android app bundle is a better way to package your app from Google
- Binary size woes from Uber
- Engineering an Uber app under 5 Megabytes from Uber
- App size matters from Farfetch
- Effect of mobile app size on Downloads from Twilio Segment
- How your APK size impacts install conversion rates from Google
- Reducing the Messenger iOS codebase from 1.7M to 360K lines of code from Facebook
- Shrinking our Android app size by 30% from The Guardian
- Reducing Android app size by 65% from PregBuddy
- App thinning, Bitcode, Slicing: an iOS tutorial

Resources for this chapter:
go.mobileatscale.com/39

CLOSING THOUGHTS

Since the launch of the iOS and Android app stores in 2008, the importance and impact of mobile apps has been steadily increasing. Many businesses increasingly depend on apps used by the majority of their customers, and several successful companies have been built on top of a single, massively successful app.

Though the importance of mobile apps has grown steadily, we are still learning about many of the challenges of how to build — and maintain — these apps at scale. How do you ensure an app works reliably for millions of daily users, while also innovating faster than your competition? How do you move quickly, and avoid stepping on each other's toes with dozens of engineers building the same app?

Some mobile engineering challenges are unique to this field. Most of the uniqueness has to do with binaries distributed through the app store, mobile devices frequently going offline, deeplinks, in-app-purchases and other topics we discussed in Part 1.

Engineers building thick client Windows, Mac or Linux apps are the closest to relate to such difficulties; as many of these challenges are unbeknown to web or backend engineers. However, very few thick client apps see as many users as mobile apps, or new versions going out as frequently — and seamlessly — as apps, or need to worry about unreliable networking as much as mobile has to.

Many engineering challenges are similar to what other teams working at scale face. Building and shipping an app used by millions in a reliable way, but also moving quickly, is a similar challenge that large-scale backend or web teams experience. Similarly, finding ways for a large team working on a single codebase to work well is nothing new.

Both the difficulties and the solutions discussed in Part 2 and Part 3 are similar to how other, non-mobile engineering teams tackle similar scale problems.

The real challenge is how many mobile engineers and managers often find themselves working on the largest client they have ever tackled, thanks to the fast adoption of mobile apps. Apart from resources in this book, one of the best things you can do is to connect with other engineers, managers and teams working on similar challenges at other companies. The discussion forums at the Mobile Native Foundation is a great place to start.

The changing languages and frameworks pose a unique challenge at this point in time. Parallel to Swift and Kotlin gaining traction for native development, we are seeing a new wave of promising cross-platform approaches emerge. Kotlin Multiplatform Mobile, Flutter and React Native and other approaches are all gaining varying levels of momentum, and offer different tradeoffs.

There has never been so many different ways to build mobile apps as there are now. Part 4 explored this landscape in-depth.

I urge you to not copy what other companies are doing or writing about, but to understand the tradeoffs between the approaches, and to identify the priorities and constraints for your team and company.

Building world-class mobile applications brings another long set of challenges. Best-in-class mobile apps have excellent performance on a variety of devices, work reliably for almost all users, and are secure and compliant. They are also built in ways that allows the team to move fast and experiment with new features without breaking the experience.

Teams use feature flags and experimentation, monitoring and alerting, and on-call as tools and processes to get here. Part 5 discussed the approaches best-in-class engineering teams employ in building apps.

Building versus buying tools is becoming an increasingly important decision. Building large-scale mobile apps is still a relatively new field, and it can be hard to find tools or vendor solutions for all the challenges you face. At Uber, we built many of our solutions in-house; from a custom CI/CD system, to a localization service, and our custom feature flagging system.

Building and maintaining functionality that is not a core part of your business does slow you down over time, though. At Uber, there are still large teams maintaining all the custom tooling that allows the mobile team to move fast. And if your company is not Uber, you might not have the scale to support this type of upfront investment.

Buying solutions is increasingly what many large companies are shifting to. More and more vendors are starting to serve apps at scale, many of these vendors founded by or employing people who used to work on the exact same challenges in-house at other firms.

The biggest reason you want to do mobile engineering right is because of the impact mobile apps have on their respective businesses. While researching this book, I have talked with several heads of mobile engineering from hypergrowth startups, to some of the biggest mobile apps in the world. They all told me the same thing.

Most businesses are seeing more and more people use their mobile apps, and this is especially true for world-class mobile apps that are fast, convenient, and reliable. The largest companies are seeing customers shift to using their apps over their website and other channels, but *only* if the app has the functionality they need, when they need it. Several companies mentioned customer retention and customer spend being higher among app users than those who do not (yet) use apps.

All of these companies are asking their mobile teams to build more features, to do this faster, and to keep quality high. They are seeing the value in mobile apps and are ready to invest in more: more people, more budget for tooling, more resources, in order to make this happen.

The mobile engineering landscape keeps changing, so keep your ear on the ground. I believe we are still at an exciting and promising time for mobile engineering. The solutions that will become industry-standard tools have either yet to be built, or are being put together as we speak.

Stay curious. Connect with industry peers. Talk about how they are solving problems that you also have. Join mobile communities, meetups, conferences, in order to keep up with where the industry is headed.

The Mobile Native Foundation was created after several teams and companies realized they were all solving the same problems, but in silos. The foundation is home to a growing number of projects on mobile tooling, and interesting discussions that are worth following and participating in. If you are interested in learning more about mobile challenges at scale, I suggest you join this community. I am already a member.

Thank you for reading this book, and if you have feedback or comments on the contents, you can reach me at scale@pragmaticengineer.com.

If you've enjoyed this book, please check out other books I've written, and feel free to connect with me at go.mobileatscale.com/connect.

- Gergely Orosz

Made in the USA
Middletown, DE
31 August 2022

72839523R00136